Today!!
Happy Birthday!
CHIC
Have a GORGEOUS DAY!
For a Special Mum
happy birthday

Crafting Cross Stitch Cards

Sue Cook

David and Charles

For Anna, our shining star.

A DAVID & CHARLES BOOK

David & Charles is an
F+W Publications Inc. company
4700 East Galbraith Road
Cincinnati, OH 45236

First published in the UK in 2007
Reprinted 2007

A catalogue record for this book is available from the British Library.

ISBN 13: 978-0-7153-2323-6 hardback
ISBN 10: 0-7153-2323-7 hardback

ISBN 13: 978-0-7153-2711-1 paperback
ISBN 10: 0-7153-2711-9 paperback

Printed in China by Shenzhen Donnelley Printing Co Ltd
for David & Charles
Brunel House Newton Abbot Devon

Executive Editor Cheryl Brown
Desk Editor Bethany Dymond
Senior Designer Charly Bailey
Project Editor and Chart Preparation Lin Clements
Production Controller Ros Napper

Visit our website at www.davidandcharles.co.uk

David & Charles books are available from all good bookshops; alternatively you can contact our Orderline on 0870 9908222 or write to us at FREEPOST EX2 110, D&C Direct, Newton Abbot, TQ12 4ZZ (no stamp required UK only); US customers call 800-289-0963 and Canadian customers call 800-840-5220.

CONTENTS

Introduction

Most of us have childhood memories of happy hours spent painting, sticking and snipping away at coloured paper. Paper chains, cards and wobbly Easter chicks are all projects I can remember proudly presenting to my parents down the years. Now I help my grandson, Sam, make things for another generation to treasure. As the pace of life grows ever more hectic, the time we spend enjoying our hobbies gives us the breathing space we need.

There has been a resurgence in crafts as a result of this, with more and more choice of materials and techniques becoming available.

The idea for this book came from my desire to combine cross stitch with new card-making techniques. Most importantly, I wanted to open up the colourful treasure trove of paper-crafting materials to readers, whether beginners or lifetime fans of cross stitch. So here you will find lots of exciting but simple techniques to bring your cross stitched cards bang up to date. Don't worry if you are new to cross stitching or card making because all the information you need to get started can be found in the Crafting Cards and Stitch Basics sections that follow.

Memorable Days, Birthday Bonanza and Seasonal Favourites are bursting with bright designs for you to stitch for friends and family. There are traditional and contemporary styles, with plenty of extra motifs to choose from in the More Card Ideas section following each of the chapters. As well as cards you will find tags and keepsakes to inspire you, all with easy-to-follow instructions ensuring a professional look you can be proud of – simply stitch the designs following the advice in Stitch Basics and then make up and embellish as described in the project instructions. Many of the motifs use only a few threads and scraps of fabric, making them perfect, portable projects. Stitch them up during your lunch hour or in a quiet time at the end of a busy day to help you unwind. If you are short on time you can mount the designs in commercially available aperture cards in the traditional way, however, my hope is that the ideas provided in this book will help you gain the confidence to be more creative in your cross stitch card making. You will soon discover that the wide range of materials available make it very easy to produce lovely cards quickly and easily.

It's been enormously enjoyable to put this book together, sourcing exciting materials, dreaming up the designs and suggesting ways to make your lovely stitching the star of any card you make. I hope I can convey some of my enthusiasm for both cross stitch and card making in its pages. The creative possibilities are only just beginning!

Crafting Cards

The idea behind this book is to help you to be more inventive about presenting your cross stitch designs, to make your embroidery the star of the show and display it to best advantage. A walk around a craft store today reveals an amazing treasure trove of ideas on how to enhance our stitching with some of the gorgeous paper products available and this book will show you how easily you can achieve some beautiful and impressive effects.

Choosing Paper and Card

There is a huge choice of totally irresistible paper and cardstock today, making it incredibly easy to build up a stock of favourites, which are sure to inspire your cross stitch card making. Some of the nicest and most varied are those designed for scrapbooking and these often form part of a themed collection featuring an attractive range of co-ordinating patterns and colours.

Remember though, to choose your paper carefully. Does it blend with or echo the colours in your stitching? Is the pattern the right scale or theme to complement your design? If you fall madly in love with a certain paper keep it for a future more appropriate project and look out for a design to go with it. Your lovely stitching must always be the star of any card you make – everything else is just the supporting act!

Special-effects These papers and cards are available in all sorts of realistic finishes like sand, pebbles, clouds and leaves and have a really contemporary look. I used a brick-effect paper for the Skater Boy on page 53 (see below).

Mulberry paper This beautiful handmade paper is available in most colours. I used pastel shades to give a soft touch to more traditional cross stitch designs and bright pinks, violets and acid greens to add a zing to cards.

Textured This is wonderful for adding interest and a three-dimensional look. The paper or card is available rippled, wood-grained, in animal skin textures and much more!

Holographic, metallic and glitter These are great for adding glitzy highlights. They are often self-adhesive. I used a silver holographic paper for Anchors Away on page 32 (see below).

This brick effect paper, used for the Skater Boy card on page 53, gives a realistic effect that is enhanced by the lettering, which has been arranged like graffiti.

Vellum This is a lovely translucent paper with a smooth finish, available in a variety of shades, patterns and embossed textures. Lightweight vellum is easy to cut, score and fold.

Decorative paper These papers are coloured and patterned in a myriad of beautiful ways. I've used various patterned papers throughout the book, such as pretty pink gingham paper for Tutu-tastic on page 28 and some striking harlequin paper for the Noble Knight on page 58.

Tearing Techniques

Tearing is so easy and can give a natural, handmade feel to your cards. I used torn mulberry paper on the wedding card on page 21 for a unique feathered effect.

Tearing paper Tear the paper towards you to open up the layers. If the paper or card is coloured on one side you will create a white torn edge. Paper vellum can be torn in the same way.

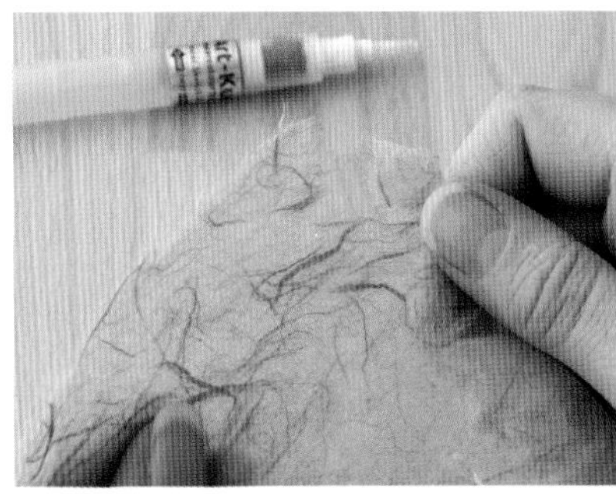

Tearing mulberry paper Damp the edges with a small paintbrush and pull the fibres away gently for a luxurious, feathered effect.

Choosing Embellishments

There is a huge array of gorgeous embellishments available to crafters. I used items such as lace, self-adhesive ribbons, diamantes, stick-on jewels, flowers, filigree stars, beads, pearl strings, felt and even craft foam, but a visit to your local craft shop or a browse of websites will uncover a much bigger treasure trove!

It's great fun collecting all sorts of embellishments and storing them ready for inspiration. Look out for themed packs of embellishments for scrapbooking too. Buttons, charms and stick-on jewels are perfect for enhancing cross stitch. Consider investing in some decorative punches like the daisy and fleur-de-lys ones I've used. These allow you stamp out co-ordinating or contrasting details to highlight your cards as well as using up any scraps you may have.

Many embellishments are self-adhesive but others can be attached with double-sided tape, craft glue or micro glue dots.

Crafty Tip

Look out for lots of goodies on sale more cheaply at the end of a season, such as Christmas. A good time to stock up.

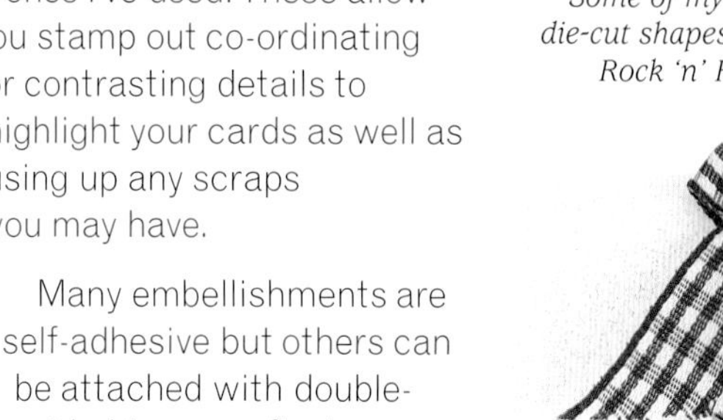

Some of my favourite embellishments are die-cut shapes. These are used to decorate the Rock 'n' Roll Fifties card on page 95.

Gorgeous self-adhesive ribbons and bows are available in a wide range of patterns and colours and it is so simple to attach them. This red gingham ribbon from the Present From Santa tag on page 92 gives a wonderful festive effect.

Themed charms and embelishments are perfect for personalising cards to suit the recipient. The ballet themed charms used in the Tutu-tastic! card on page 28 are ideal for a keen dancer.

Basic Kit

For the cards and keepsakes in this book you will need a collection of basic equipment.

- **Pencils and erasers** – use sharp HB pencils and a teardrop-shaped eraser.
- **Rulers** – use a plastic ruler for measuring and a metal ruler for cutting out. A set square will also be useful.
- **Cutting mat and craft knife** – for accurate cutting.
- **Scissors** – use general scissors for paper and card, fine-pointed scissors with longer blades for cutting out motifs and deckle scissors for decorative effects.
- **Embossing tool and bone folder** – very useful for creasing and folding cards from cardstock.
- **Adhesive tapes and glues** – double-sided tape, clear glue or PVA and glue dots are all useful.
- **Foam pads** – to give a raised look to your work.
- **Tracing paper** – will be needed for transferring templates (or use ordinary greaseproof paper).
- **Tweezers** – ideal for positioning very small items.
- **Shaped punches and single hole punch** – for punching shapes such as flowers, moons, stars and punching holes in tags and creating circles for decoration.
- **Needles** – use tapestry needles for cross stitching, 'sharps' for general sewing and a darning needle for making holes.
- **Cross stitch fabrics** – Aida and evenweaves have been used for the projects, mostly in white and cream shades.
- **Cross stitch threads** – I've used the DMC range of stranded cotton (floss) but if you prefer Anchor ask at your local needlecraft store. Some metallic threads were also used.

Using Iron-On Adhesive

Stitched motifs can be made much more adaptable if you prepare them by applying iron-on adhesive to the back to prevent fraying. I use Therm O Web HeatnBond ® ultra-hold iron-on adhesive: sold in 1yd packs, it is available from most large craft suppliers and is simple and economical to use. It works with most fabrics but test on a scrap first. Always apply the adhesive to fabric *after* stitching, not before. The adhesive can also be used to attach an embroidery to another piece of fabric. Remove the paper, place the motif right side up and iron in the same way.

1 Neaten the back of your stitching by trimming loose threads and then cut out a piece of the adhesive slightly larger than your stitched piece.

2 Pre-heat an iron to silk setting (no steam). Place the adhesive paper-side (smooth) up on wrong side of fabric.

3 Hold the iron on the paper side of the adhesive for two seconds and then glide the iron in an overlapping motion across the area until the entire surface has bonded. Allow to cool. I find it easier to cut out the motif with the paper backing still in place.

Cutting Out Motifs

Cutting out motifs once they have been backed with adhesive is a simple way to decorate a single-fold card and very effective if creating a card with more than one element or layer. It's worth taking time to master this technique because it allows you much greater flexibility in using cross stitch designs. It frees you from having to use aperture cards to display your work and makes your cross stitch much more versatile.

1 To make cutting easier, first trim away the bulk of excess fabric. Start cutting at the widest point of the motif, positioning the scissors carefully. Cut slowly and steadily, moving the fabric as much as possible to avoid having to re-position the scissors too often.

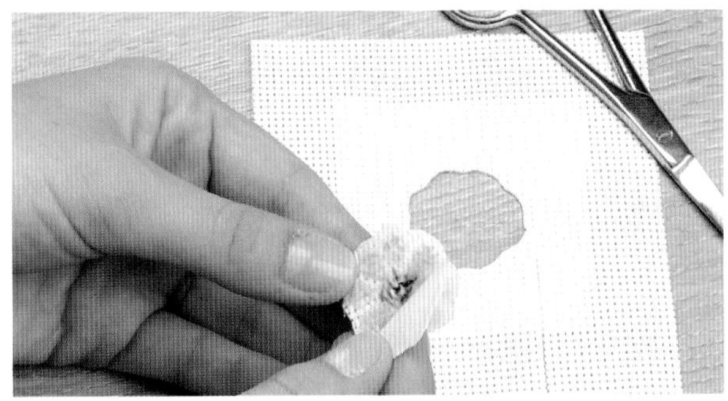

2 Once your motif is cut out, peel away the backing paper. The adhesive will not be sticky as it only activated by heat. One or two threads may need to be trimmed using embroidery scissors. The adhesive will have stabilized the stitches and the fabric threads and reduce the liklihood of the edges fraying.

Some designs are cut out closely following the stitching line, as shown by the house design, while others are trimmed in a more freehand style to reflect the curves of a particular motif, as shown by the ghost. The best look is achieved by leaving just one or two Aida squares (two to four evenweave threads) around the stitching.

Using Ready-Made Cards

Pre-scored cards ensure a professional finish every time and are available in a huge array of colours, finishes and shapes. There are single-fold cards, with and without windows or apertures, and double-fold cards with apertures, where a section of the card folds over to cover the back of the stitching. The colour of the card and the shape of the aperture can make a great deal of difference to the look of your finished stitching. Make sure the aperture is large enough for the design. Consider the shape of your project too – would it be best in a square, oval or circular aperture?

If you want to make your projects up as shown in the book refer to the card suppliers on page 104. Most have websites with advice and inspiration.

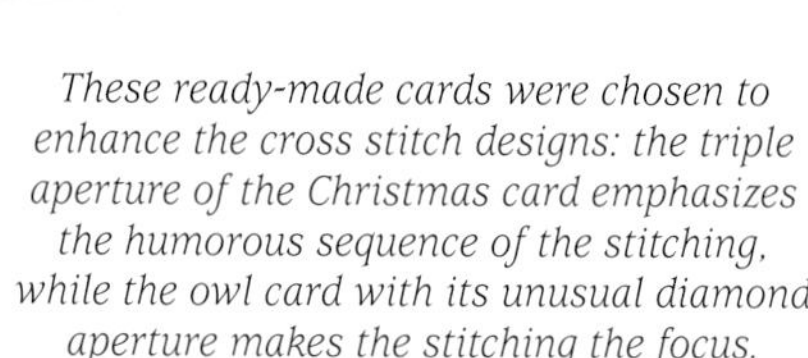

These ready-made cards were chosen to enhance the cross stitch designs: the triple aperture of the Christmas card emphasizes the humorous sequence of the stitching, while the owl card with its unusual diamond aperture makes the stitching the focus.

Mounting Stitching into an Aperture Card

Commercial cards with apertures are a quick way to display cross stitch designs. Where I've used cards with pre-cut apertures I've given measurements but if you are stitching a motif from the extra motif sections or altering the main project, check your own card sizes.

1 Lay the card face up on the stitching with the design centred in the aperture. Put a pin in each corner of the stitching to mark the aperture. Remove the card. Trim the embroidery to fit behind the aperture with a 2cm (¾in) border. Remove pins.

2 On the wrong side of the card, stick double-sided tape round the aperture. Peel off the backing. A narrow tape can be bent around oval or circular apertures.

3 Lay the stitching face down centrally on top of the aperture and press firmly. For a padded look, add a piece of wadding (batting) on top of the stitching. Now run more double-sided tape around all edges of the centre portion and peel off the backing tape.

4 Fold the left side of the card over the back of the stitching. Use a bone folder to press all edges down firmly. Add embellishments to your card as desired.

Making Your Own Cards

If you are unable to find a suitable pre-folded card, it's easy to make your own from cardstock. Choose your card carefully and buy the best you can afford, and thick enough to support your stitching (between 160–240gm) – nothing is worse than a lovely card that keeps falling over! Make sure the colour or finish doesn't overwhelm your stitching, which should always be the main feature of the card.

1 Once you have cut your chosen card to size using a metal ruler and craft knife on a cutting mat, measure and mark where you want the fold to be. Align a metal ruler or paper trimmer between these two points and, holding firmly, pull an embossing tool down it using light pressure. The embossed line or 'mountain' fold will be on the inside of the card.

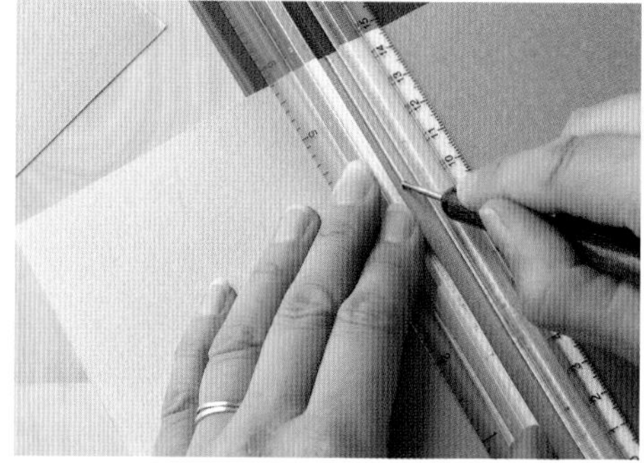

2 Align the edges of the card and use a bone folder to flatten the crease.

Crafty Tip

Try using scissors with a deckle or decorative edge to trim your card or paper elements – this will add an extra visual dimension to your card.

Layering Elements

Layering different elements, such as card or decorative paper adds interest to your card projects. See for example the Birthday Princess card on page 52 and the Noble Knight card on page 58. You can buy card and paper in blocks, often themed with patterns and colours that work beautifully together. They can be used straight off the block or trimmed to size. Use double-sided tape or micro glue dots to mount the layers.

1 Attach double-sided tape to the edges of the element to be stuck to your card. Pull back just a little of the backing tape so the tabs are visible from the front.

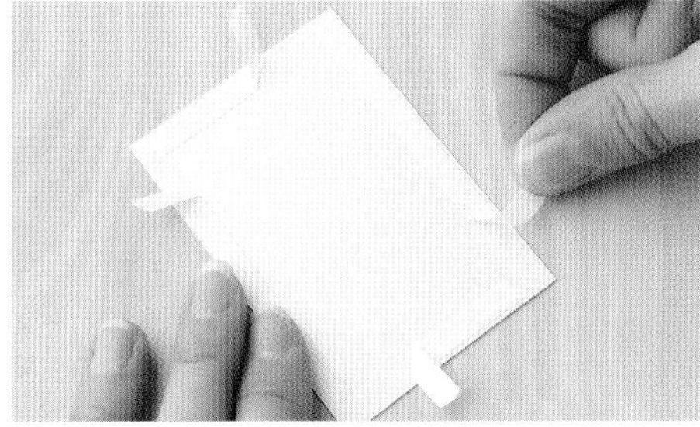

2 Position the element on the card, moving the layer around until you are happy with the position. Firm down where the tape is exposed.

3 Peel the backing paper away completely and firmly press down all the edges.

Adding Text

Adding text to your card always gives it that wonderful hand-crafted look and makes the card much more personal to the recipient. There are many ways to add text to your projects – here are some I used.

Hand written If you have good handwriting there are lots of super pens available to use with cards. Some of the nicest are the fine-tipped gel pens that have a lovely subtle metallic finish in a huge choice of colours.

Stick-on alphabets There is a huge variety of these available in lots of eye-catching styles and colours, most of which are self-adhesive. I've used several in this book but my favourites are the 'jelly' letters that have a slightly domed or 'pebble' effect. Most come in packs of upper and lower case letters but make sure the size is right for your card.

Peel-offs These normally come in themed sheets and it's easy to find something to suit most occasions. The sheets often contain other motifs, such as borders or decorative corners, making them good value.

Rub-ons As the name suggests these are simply cut out from the backing sheet, positioned on your card and rubbed down using a little tool supplied with them. Like peel-offs they often contain a combination of text and motifs on the same theme.

Computer printed As many people now have access to a computer I've included a few designs with text generated by a fonts package. These are often supplied as part of your computer start-up software bundle. They are now reasonably priced and are usually including in greetings card software. Producing text in this way allows you to experiment with different typefaces, scales and colour. If you have a PC and intend making a lot of cards it is worth investing in a fonts package to give a professional look to your projects.

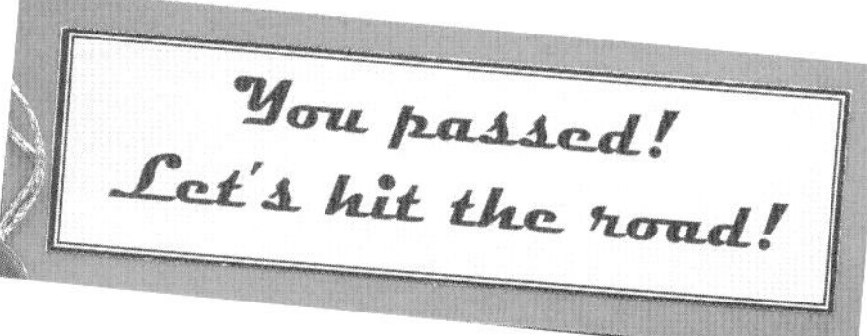

Fabulous Fonts

You can create different moods with your cards by choosing appropriate fonts for your greetings. Here are some examples.

Try Fette Fraktur LT Std or Didot for traditional festive greetings.

Merry Christmas

HAPPY NEW YEAR

Comic Sans or Khaki Std are good for a friendly birthday greeting.

Have a Great Day!

It's Your Birthday!

How about using Decaying to get in the mood for Hallowe'en?

HAVE A SCARY HALLOWE'EN!

Crafty Tip

If you collect a varied selection of text and decorative elements and store them in a box, you will never be short of inspiration when choosing a greeting for a particular card.

Stitch Basics

This section contains all the basic stitching information that you will need to stitch the designs in this book – see page 6 for the basic kit required.

Tip-Top Techniques

When stitching the designs these useful pointers will help you produce excellent work.

- Before starting, check the design size given with each project and make sure that this is the size you require for your finished embroidery.
- Fabric should be at least 5cm (2in) larger all round than the finished stitching, to allow for making up.
- Find and mark the centre of the fabric, in order to stitch the design centrally on the fabric. To find the centre, fold the fabric in half horizontally and then vertically, then tack (baste) along the folds (or use tailor's chalk). The centre point is where the two lines meet. This point on the fabric should correspond to the centre point on the chart. Remove lines on completion of the work.
- Avoid using knots when starting and finishing as this will make your work lumpy when mounted.
- Work cross stitch with two strands over one block of Aida or over two threads of evenweave. For neat work, the top stitch of each of the cross stitches should all face the same direction. Work backstitches and French knots with one strand, unless otherwise instructed.
- Always add a backstitch outline after the cross stitch has been completed to prevent the line being broken.
- Measurements are given in metric with imperial conversions in brackets – work with one or the other. Ready-made card sizes are given in millimetres as most manufacturers use this measurement.
- If you want to work the design on a different count fabric you will need to re-calculate the finished size. Divide the numbers of stitches in the design by the fabric count number, e.g., 140 stitches high x 140 wide ÷ 14-count = a design size of 10 x 10in (25.5 x 25.5cm). Working on evenweave usually means working over two threads, so divide the fabric count by two before you start calculating.

Working the Stitches

Starting and finishing stitching Bring the needle up at the start of the first stitch, leaving a 2.5cm (1in) 'tail' at the back. Secure the tail by working the first few stitches over it. Start new threads by first passing the needle through several stitches on the back.

To finish off thread, pass the needle through some nearby stitches on the back of the work and then trim the thread.

Backstitch Backstitches give definition and outline areas. Use one strand of thread unless otherwise instructed. Follow Fig 1, bringing the needle up at 1 and down at 2, up at 3, down at 4, and so on.

You will see that some of the designs throughout the book use a 'sketchy' backstitch style, with some longer backstitches that do not follow the diagram so closely.

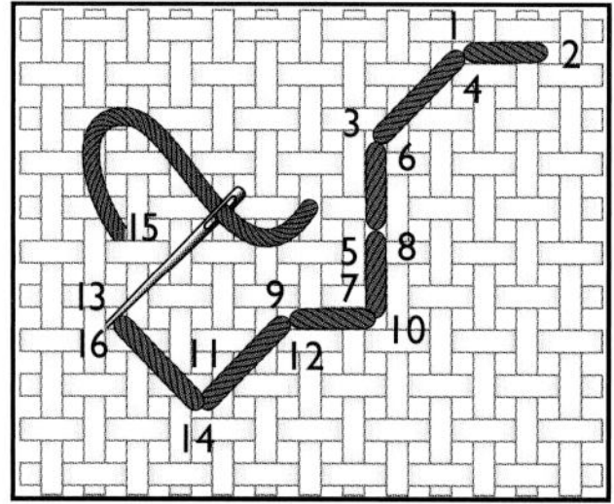

Fig 1 Working backstitch

Cross stitch A cross stitch can be worked singly or a number of half stitches can be sewn in a line and completed on the return journey. Use two strands of thread unless otherwise instructed.

To make a cross stitch over one block of Aida, follow the sequence in Fig 2a – up at 1, down at 2, up at 3, down at 4. Work cross stitch on evenweave in the same way but over two fabric threads, as in Fig 2b.

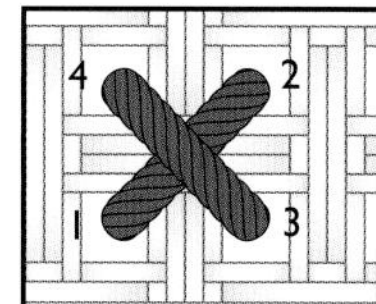

Fig 2a Working a single cross stitch on Aida

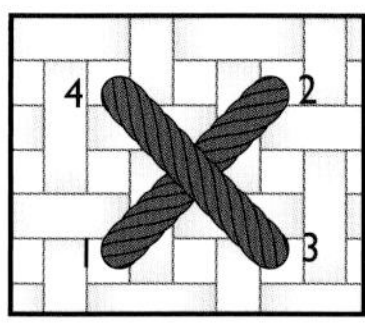

Fig 2b Working a single cross stitch on evenweave

Using Charts and Keys

Colour charts are provided for all projects. The motifs in the More Card Ideas sections share a key on each spread, so check which colours you need.

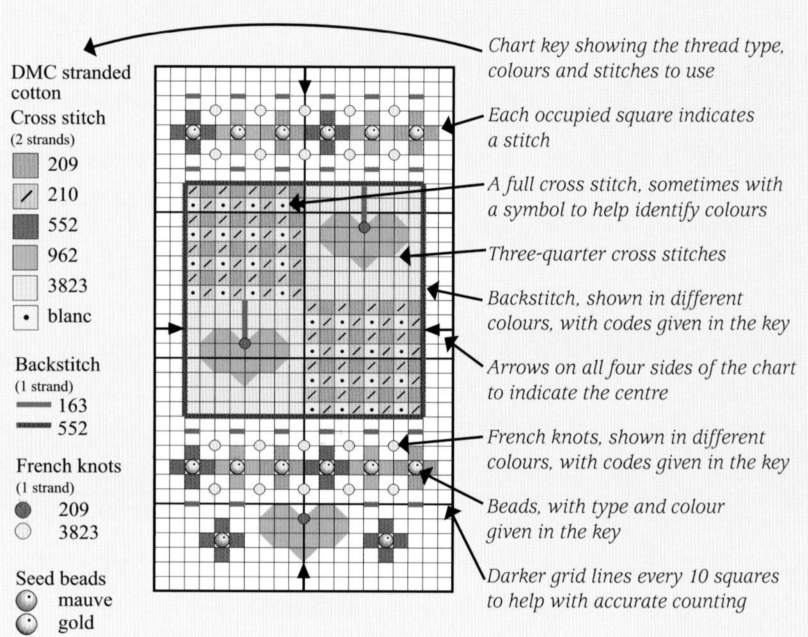

Three-quarter cross stitch These give more detail to a design and are shown by a triangle in a square on charts. They are easiest to work on evenweave (see Fig 3). To work on Aida, make a quarter stitch from the corner into the centre of the square, piercing the Aida, then work a half stitch across the other diagonal.

Fig 3 Working three-quarter cross stitch

Long stitch This is used in some projects and is useful for working stars. Work a long, straight stitch starting and finishing at the points on the chart.

French knots These have been used as eye and nose details in some designs. Use one strand of thread unless otherwise instructed. To work, follow Fig 4, bringing the needle and thread up through the fabric where the knot is to be positioned. Wrap the thread twice around the needle, holding the thread firmly close to the needle. Twist the needle back through the fabric close to where it first emerged. Holding the knot down carefully, pull the thread through to the back leaving the knot neatly on the surface.

Fig 4 Working a French knot

Three quarters cross stitch is used in My First Album on page 15 to give more definition to the heart shape (left). The baby's face has been made up from full cross stich, which creates a more jagged edge.

Attaching beads I've used seed beads to enhance some cards and bring sparkle to the cross stitch. Some motifs could be stitched either completely or partly in beads. To do this, simply substitute areas of stitching for beads of a similar colour. Seed beads are so easy to attach, using sewing thread matching the fabric colour, a beading needle or very fine 'sharp' needle and a half cross stitch.

I used clusters of gold seed beads (above) to bring an extra sparkle to the Cross of Gold card on page 17.

Crafty Tip

When working with seed beads, put them in an egg cup – the smooth, slightly curved sides will make it easier to pick up a bead on the point of your needle.

Adapting the Designs

I hope that the projects in this book will inspire you to create your own ideas – here are a few suggestions for adapting the designs.

Use the motif in other ways
I've given some alternative ideas throughout each chapter but use your imagination to expand these. For example, add the saucy forties cocktail waitress to a bag for lingerie or the frustrated fisherman to a photo album for an angler. If you're into scrapbooking, you can also use cross stitch motifs to embellish pages. Try adding motifs to clothing, bags or cushions using iron-on adhesive.

Mix and match motifs It is possible to combine motifs or substitute one part of a motif for another but it's best to chart the new design on graph paper before starting to stitch.

Change the size of a design
Changing the finished size of a design is easily done by working on a different fabric count. The higher the count, the smaller the finished design will be, and vice versa. So, if you want to work a design smaller, say to fit into a coaster, stitch it on 16- or 18-count Aida instead of 14-count. See calculating design size in the panel opposite (final point).

Change the fabric colour This can have a major impact but make sure that the thread colours aren't too similar to the new fabric colour. I have mainly used white or cream shades, which allowed me to co-ordinate or contrast the design colours with the card and other embellishments. Give motifs on coloured fabric the simplest treatment perhaps using just a textured cream or white card to display them.

Memorable Days

In this chapter you'll find a card or gift idea to mark most of life's major celebrations. As well as inspirational card ideas, I've included a sprinkling of special keepsakes destined to become cherished reminders of wonderful days. A pretty album for baby's first pictures, a delicate floral wedding ring pillow and a Tiffany-inspired memory book for a golden anniversary are all impressive but easy to make.

Quick-to-stitch cards are useful additions to this chapter and small enough for last-minute stitching. Make one for a new baby or to celebrate passing a driving test. Lovely tags will enhance your christening, new home or wedding gifts. Larger cards use a variety of finishing techniques and will ensure that friends and relatives are thrilled to receive them. As well as births, weddings and special anniversaries, you'll find engagement, graduation and bon voyage cards. There's even a special design to mark the beginning of a whole new life in another country, which is sure to be kept as a reminder of the old one.

Dip into the wide selection of additional motifs charted on pages 34–43 to find even more ideas for your memorable days stitching.

CHAMPAGNE

Just married
Best Wishes on your Wedding day

To have and To hold...
28th May 2006

CONGRATULATIONS

Hello Baby Boy

You will need

14-count cream Aida 15cm (6in) square

DMC stranded cotton (floss) as listed in chart key

Single-fold card 105 x 150mm (4 x 6in) in pale blue

Iron-on adhesive

Two safety pin embellishments

Die-cut teddy bear shape 55mm

Padded 6mm heart in red (optional)

Stitch count 44h x 48w
Design size 8 x 8.7cm (3⅛ x 3½in)

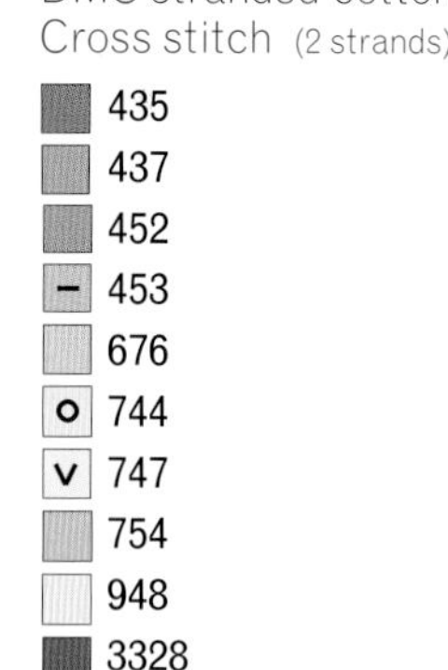

Backstitch (1 strand)
— 838

Note Stitch the motifs separately if you have fabric scraps to use up. The same design for a girl is shown in a pink colourway in More Card Ideas on page 34.

To craft the card

Iron the adhesive on the back of the stitching (see page 7). Cut out the lettering and then the Moses basket, leaving two empty squares all round. Referring to the picture, arrange the various elements of the card, or choose your own layout. Use double-sided tape to attach the stitched designs to the card. Attach the teddy and safety pins using mini glue dots. Add a sweet finishing touch with a tiny padded heart on the teddy.

My First Album

You will need

28-count white evenweave 18 x 20cm (7 x 8in)

DMC stranded cotton (floss) as listed in chart key

Pink keepsake album 13 x 18cm (5 x 7in) (see Suppliers)

Spatter-foam mesh (optional) 10 x 17cm (4 x 6¾in) in pink

Four pink embroidered daisies (optional)

Stitch count 42h x 70w
Design size 7.6 x 12.7cm (3 x 5in)

To craft the card Measure 6mm (¼in) beyond the widest points of the design on all sides. Mark this cutting line with a row of soft pencil dots. Cut out and fray the fabric edge up to the stitched border. Pink spatter foam mesh gives an extra pretty look to the album cover. Use strips of double-sided tape in the centre of the mesh and attach it to the album cover. Stick the stitched piece on top with more tape. Use mini glue dots to add the daisies (cut from a strip).

DMC stranded cotton

Cross stitch (2 strands)

209	725	838	957	blanc
211	727	948	959	
415	754	956	964	

Backstitch (1 strand)
- 838

French knots (1 strand)
- 838

Birth Card

I've used the tiny baby motif from page 34 in this card with a circular aperture. Self-adhesive 'jelly' letters are a great way to add greetings, using the embossed edge of the circle as a guide to placing them. Finish off with tiny lilac daisies. The colours of this card make it perfect to stitch up in advance of a birth. Change the shades if you want it specifically for a boy or girl and stitch two babies for twins. This motif is also suitable for a gift tag.

Little Lamb

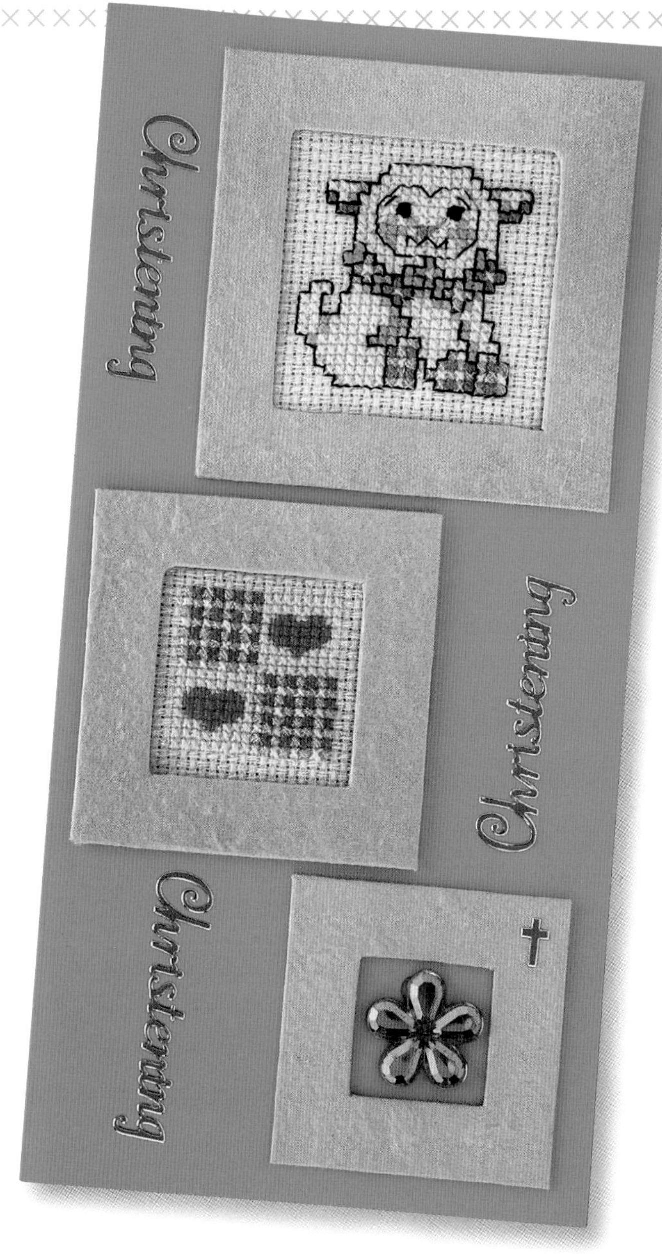

You will need

14-count pearl lustre Aida 10cm (4in) square

DMC stranded cotton (floss) as listed in chart key

Single-fold card 105 x 210mm (4 x 8¼in) in pale aqua

Iron-on adhesive

Three mulberry paper 'window frames' in toning pastel colours in large, medium and small (see Suppliers)

One large flower gem in pale pink

Three silver christening stickers and tiny silver cross from same sheet

Stitch count 22h x 42w
Design size 4 x 7.6cm (1½ x 3in)

Note You can use the measurements above if stitching the motifs on a single piece of Aida, or stitch the motifs separately if you have fabric scraps to use up.

To craft the card Iron the adhesive on the back of the stitching (see page 7). Trim the motifs to fit the paper window frames and stick behind the frames using double-sided tape. Refer to the picture or arrange your own layout then use glue dots to attach the three frames to the card. Stick a flower gem into the smallest frame, and then add the christening stickers and tiny cross as shown.

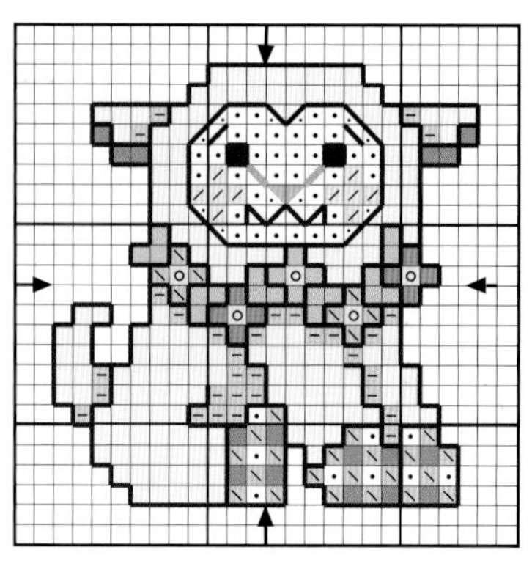

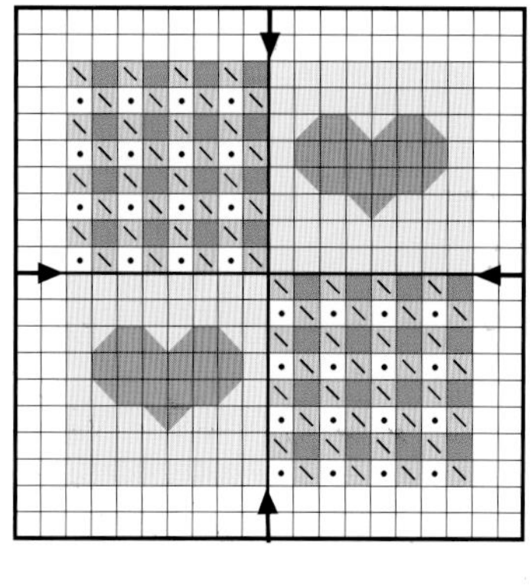

DMC stranded cotton
Cross stitch (2 strands)

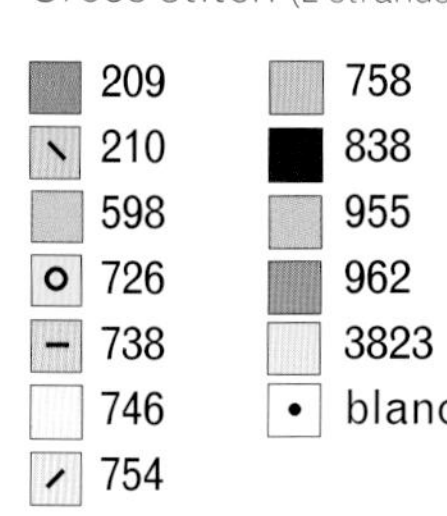

209
210
598
726
738
746
754
758
838
955
962
3823
blanc

Backstitch (1 strand)

758
838

Use this card as a birth congratulations or a first birthday card. Add your own lettering and look out for baby-themed embellishments to fit the smallest frame.

Add the baby's photo to one of the frames for a keepsake touch.

Cross of Gold

You will need

14-count pearl-lustre Aida 10 x 13cm (4 x 5in)

DMC Light Effects thread E3821

Gold seed beads

Double-fold card 90 x 119mm (3½ x 4½in) with arched aperture 55 x 80mm (2¼ x 3¼in) in sunflower yellow

Wadding (batting) same size as finished design

Paper daisies, one white and two yellow

Gold pen (optional)

Stitch count 32h x 24w
Design size 5.8 x 4.4cm (2¼ x 1¾in)

The simple design of this cross makes it perfect as a baptism card for an older child or adult, or to celebrate a first communion. Add your lettering in gold pen.

For a bereavement card, stitch the cross in silver on plain white Aida, omitting the beads if preferred. Use a pale lilac or green card and add white flowers, finishing with your message of sympathy.

To craft the card Before assembling my card I outlined the arch with a gold pen following the embossed line around the arch. Mount the finished stitching in the card (see page 8) using the wadding for a padded look. To finish, use mini glue dots to stick the three daisies to the edge of the arch.

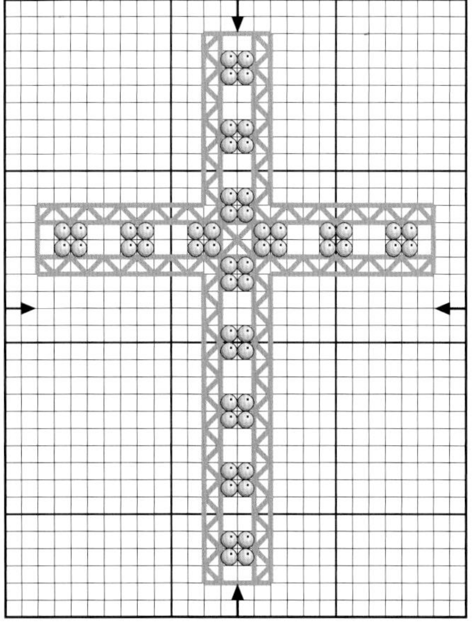

Backstitch (2 strands)
— Light Effects E3821

Seed beads
gold

Christening Tag

I used a card with a 35mm (1⅜in) square aperture and cut it down to the right size for a gift tag, stitching the sweet baby motif from page 35. Finished with a narrow gold ribbon bow and padded heart, the little daisies framing the baby make this a perfect addition to a christening gift. Use pink or blue in the motif and add matching trimmings for a customized gift tag.

What a Sparkler!

You will need

14-count cream Aida 15cm (6in) square

DMC stranded cotton (floss) as listed in chart key

Single-fold card 125mm (5in) square in pearlescent pink

Iron-on adhesive

Thin card 9.5 x 1.5cm (3¾ x ½in) in pearlescent lilac

Polka-dot paper 12.5 x 5cm (5 x 2in) in turquoise

Scissors with decorative edging

Clear self-adhesive 'jelly' letters for wording

Stitch count 55h x 53w
Design size 10 x 9.5cm (4 x 3¾in)

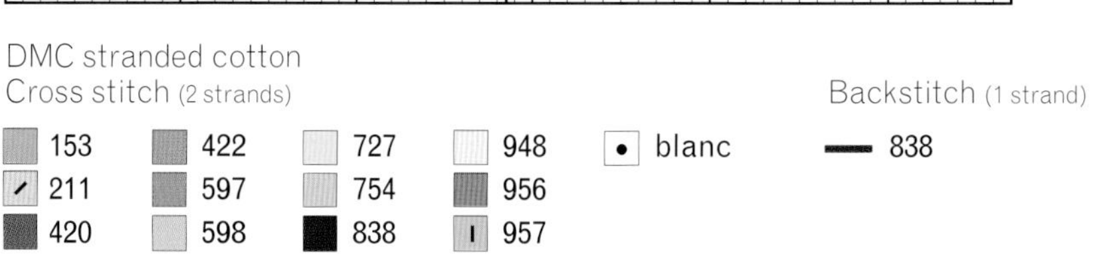

To craft the card Iron the adhesive on the back of the stitching (see page 7). Cut out the design leaving a small amount of fabric all round – aim for a curvy look and don't follow the stitching too exactly (see page 7). Use decorative scissors on one long side of the polka-dot paper for a scalloped edge. Stick the paper on the card using double-sided tape, leaving a small margin of card showing. Use jelly letters to write 'Engagement' to the piece of lilac pearlescent card – the letters can run in a different direction if you prefer. Finally, secure the stitching in place with double-sided tape.

Make It Special

You could stitch this design on a larger piece of fabric and add the names or date of the engagement, using the alphabet on page 20. It could then be framed as a little keepsake sampler.

Three Steps to Love

You will need

14-count cream Aida 20 x 9cm (8 x 3½in)

DMC stranded cotton (floss) as listed in chart key

Double-fold card 210 x 100mm (8¼ x 4in) with triple aperture in pearl white

Wadding (batting) same size as the finished design

Two padded hearts 6mm in red

Stitch count 82h x 22w
Design size 15 x 4cm (6 x 1½in)

Note Each of the apertures on this card measures 4.5cm (1¾in) square: refer to the measurements above if you want to stitch the motifs on a single piece of Aida, leaving eight squares between each motif to fit perfectly into the spaces. Alternatively, stitch the motifs separately if you have scraps of fabric to use up.

To craft the card

Mount the finished stitching in the card (see page 8) using the wadding for a padded look. To finish, attach the tiny red hearts using mini glue dots.

DMC stranded cotton
Cross stitch (2 strands)

- 320
- 368
- 415
- × 437
- 727
- 728
- 754
- 760
- 827
- 3328
- / 3713
- I 3823
- • blanc

Backstitch (1 strand)

- — 838

French knots (1 strand)

- ● 838

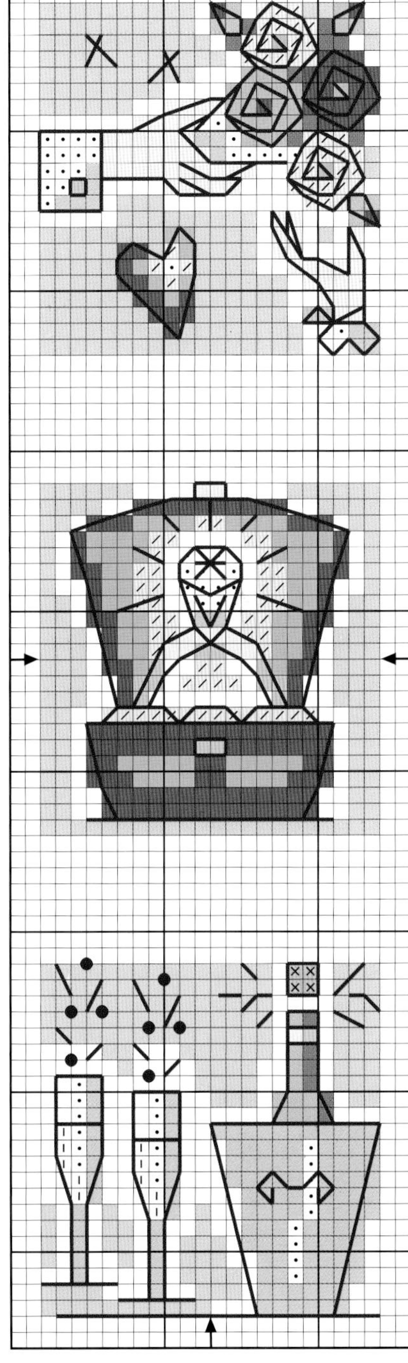

The three parts of this design could be used separately, for example, stitch the Champagne bottle and glasses as a card to celebrate any special occasion or achievement.

The ring motif could be used on a gift tag accompanying an engagement gift.

From This Day Forward...

You will need

28-count white evenweave 18cm (7in) square

DMC stranded cotton (floss) and Madeira metallic gold as listed in chart key

White backing fabric 18cm (7in) square

Small amount of polyester stuffing

Stitch count 43h x 66w
Design size 7.8 x 12cm (3 x 4¾in)

Note Use the alphabet and numbers charted below to backstitch your own dates for your own special days or to change the message. Remember to stitch over two threads of the evenweave fabric.

To craft the card Measure 4cm (1½in) from the sides of the finished design and 5cm (2in) from the top and bottom edge. Then lightly mark with a row of pencil dots – this is the cutting line and includes a seam allowance. Cut the backing fabric the same size. With right sides facing, machine sew the pieces together using a 1.25cm (½in) seam allowance. Leave a small gap at the bottom for turning. Trim seams and corners, turn through to the right side, stuff firmly and slipstitch the seam closed.

Make It Special

Use the bride's dress or bouquet colours in the floral border or substitute seed beads for the flower petals. You could also add a tassel at each corner of the pillow or trim it all round with lace. For an extra special touch, add some rose or jasmine pot-pourri to the filling.

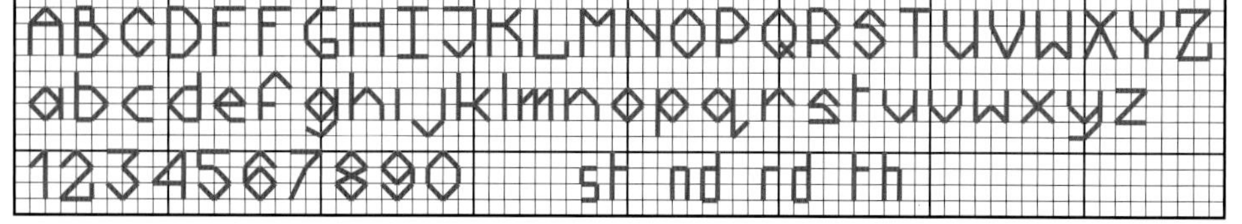

DMC stranded cotton
Cross stitch (2 strands)

- 368
- 727
- 772
- 962
- 963
- 3716
- blanc
- Madeira metallic No 20 shade 2024 gold (1 strand)

Backstitch (1 strand)

- 962
- Madeira metallic gold

French knots (1 strand)

- Madeira metallic gold

Just Married!

You will need

14-count cream Aida 13cm (5in) square

DMC stranded cotton (floss) as listed in chart key

Double-fold card 150mm (6in) square with 100mm (4in) square aperture in white linen effect

Wadding (batting) same size as finished design

Gold stickers from a sheet of wedding greetings

Small amount of confetti (optional)

Stitch count 52h x 49w
Design size 9.4 x 9cm (3¾ x 3½in)

To craft the card

Mount the finished stitching in the card (see page 8) using the wadding for a padded look. Choose your wording then place the gold stickers as shown, using the embossed line as a guide. Use a glue stick to attach a scattering of confetti if you wish, or cut shapes from scraps of coloured tissue paper.

DMC stranded cotton
Cross stitch (2 strands)

- 318
- 340
- 341
- 415
- 600
- 603
- 605
- 3855
- blanc

Backstitch (1 strand)
- 838

Wedding Tag

There are more wedding motifs in the More Card Ideas chart section on pages 36–37. This modern design from page 37 is enhanced by silk mulberry paper, feathered by damping the edges slightly. Add a tiny lilac heart button to the centre and finish with a toning tasselled twisted cord.

Retro Hearts

You will need

14-count cream Aida 14 x 15cm ($5\frac{1}{2}$ x 6in)

DMC stranded cotton (floss) as listed in chart key

Single-fold card 125mm (5in) square in pearlescent lilac

Iron-on adhesive

Flower gems in pale orange, one large and two small (optional)

Stitch count 39h x 48w
Design size 7 x 8.7cm ($2\frac{3}{4}$ x $3\frac{1}{2}$in)

To craft the card

Iron the adhesive on to the back of the stitching (see page 7). Count two squares beyond the widest points of the design on all sides and mark a cutting line with a row of soft pencil dots. Cut the design to size and using double-sided tape attach the stitching to the card, leaving a slightly larger margin at the lower edge. To complement the retro style, add the gem flowers with glue dots.

> Stitch just the large mauve hearts in a group of four for a quick gift tag.
>
> XXX
>
> Work the large mauve hearts and smaller pink hearts alternately in a vertical row for a bookmark.

DMC stranded cotton
Cross stitch (2 strands)

- 208
- 209
- 211
- 600
- 602
- 603
- 605
- 734
- 740
- 742

Backstitch (1 strand)

- 600
- 730

French knots (1 strand)

- 600

A Winning Team

You will need

14-count cream Aida 15 x 14cm (6 x 5½in)

DMC stranded cotton (floss) as listed in chart key

Single-fold card 125mm (5in) square in bright red metallic

Iron-on adhesive

Gold 'Happy Anniversary' sticker

Stitch count 36h x 45w
Design size 6.5 x 8.2cm (2½ x 3¼in)

Note The numbers on the shirts represent the year of the anniversary, to be stitched with two strands of white. Use the slightly larger numbers in the chart provided for the 'His' shirt.

To craft the card Iron the adhesive on the back of the stitching (see page 7). Count five squares beyond the widest points of the design on all sides and mark a cutting line with a row of soft pencil dots. Cut the design to size and trim the corners by cutting diagonally across five squares. Using double-sided tape attach the design to the card leaving a slightly larger margin at the lower edge. Add a gold 'Happy Anniversary' sticker to finish.

Make It Special

This is a perfect card for a couple who love football. If this isn't the right strip for their favourite team, simply change the colours and choose a card to complement them. You could embellish the card with football-themed charms.

DMC stranded cotton
Cross stitch (2 strands)

- 310
- 666
- blanc

Backstitch

- 310 (1 strand)
- blanc (2 strands)

French knots (1 strand)

- 310

1234567890
1234567890

Use these numbers to change the anniversary: backstitch in two strands of white or colour of your choice

Fountain of Silver

You will need

28-count white evenweave 13 x 10cm (5 x 4in)

DMC Light Effects threads and Madeira metallic threads as listed in chart key

Seed beads in dusky pink

Double-fold card 90 x 119mm (3½ x 4¾in) with 55 x 80mm (2⅛ x 3⅛in) arched aperture in silver linen effect

Wadding (batting) same size as finished design

Small silver envelope and card (optional)

Two small white doves (optional)

Stitch count 36h x 26w
Design size 6.5 x 4.7cm (2½ x 1¾in)

Note Remember to stitch over two threads of the evenweave fabric.

To craft the card Mount the finished stitching in the card (see page 8) using the wadding for a padded look. Assemble the small silver envelope and write the words 'Silver Wedding' on the card inside. Using glue dots, add the two white doves or your choice of embellishment.

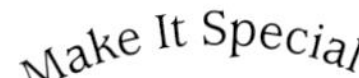

This design would look very pretty stitched completely with seed beads and mounted on the lid of a keepsake box (see the Glasgow Rose Trinket Box on page 81).

DMC Light Effects
Cross stitch (2 strands)
- E316
- E317
- E415

Backstitch (1 strand)
- Madeira metallic No.20 shade 2042

Seed beads
- dusky pink

Golden Memories

You will need

14-count cream Aida 13 x 18cm (5 x 7in)

DMC stranded cotton (floss) as listed in chart key

Mini album 13 x 18cm (5 x 7in) in leaf green (see Suppliers)

Iron-on adhesive

Piece of thin gold card with linen-effect finish 11 x 15cm (4¼ x 6in)

Golden wedding anniversary sticker and two small hearts, from same sheet

Ornate gold heart button (optional)

Stitch count 44h x 72w
Design size 8 x 13cm (3⅛ x 5⅛in)

To craft the card

Use double-sided tape to stick the piece of gold card to the front of your album. Iron the adhesive on the back of the stitching (see page 7). Trim the stitching and use double-sided tape to attach it to the gold card, positioning it about 1.25cm (½in) below the top edge, leaving a larger margin at the bottom to attach the lettering. Fix the gold heart stickers in the top corners. If your album comes with narrow ribbon, as mine did, then attach the ornate button to finish.

Instead of using stick-on lettering, add your own words or message on the album.

The design's mellow colours make it perfect for a retirement card.

Dream Cottage

You will need

14-count cream Aida 12.5cm (5in) square

DMC stranded cotton (floss) as listed in chart key

Single-fold card 145mm (5¾in) square in pale yellow

Iron-on adhesive

Piece of beige card 2.5 x 4cm (1 x 1½in)

Strip of dark brown card 5 x 0.6cm (2 x ¼in)

Paper daisies, one white and one yellow

Self-adhesive ribbon 15cm (6in) x 6mm (¼in) in pale green

Stitch count 54w x 54h
Design size 9.8cm (3⅞in) square

To craft the card Iron the adhesive on the back of the stitching (see page 7). Cut out the design leaving one square of fabric all round and attach to the card with double-sided tape, leaving a larger space at the bottom. To make the sign, write 'Sold' in red crayon on the beige card. Stick the strip of dark brown card to the sign with a glue dot. Position the sign at an angle and secure with glue dots, adding the daisies. Stick the self-adhesive ribbon along the lower edge of the card folding it over at each end for a neat finish. There is another motif in this style charted on page 40.

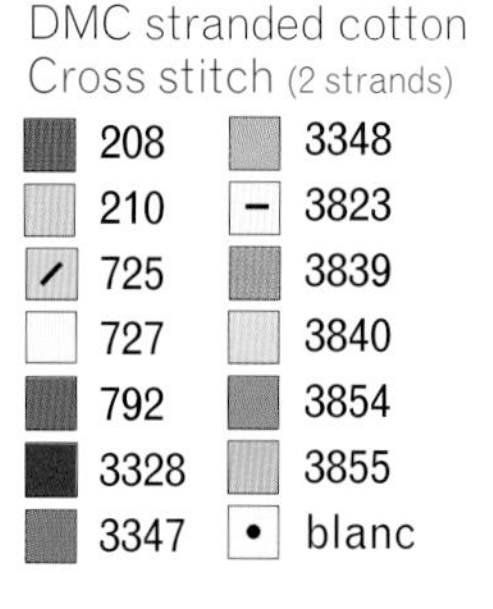

Move Along Home

You will need

28-count white evenweave 15 x 12.5cm (6 x 5in)

DMC stranded cotton (floss) as listed in chart key

Double-fold card 180 x 115mm (7 x 4½in) with 110 x 75mm (4¼ x 3in) aperture in pale lilac

Wadding (batting) same size as finished design

Self-adhesive ribbon, two 11cm (4¼in) lengths x 6mm (¼in) wide in lilac gingham

Four 6mm heart buttons in pale lilac

Stitch count 57h x 44w
Design size 10 x 8cm (4 x 3⅛in)

DMC stranded cotton
Cross stitch (2 strands)

	553	–	955
	554		3810
I	644		3853
O	740	/	3854
	747		3855
	913	•	blanc

Backstitch (1 strand)
— 838

French knots (1 strand)
● 838

Note Remember to stitch over two threads of the evenweave fabric.

To craft the card Mount your finished stitching in the card (see page 8) using the wadding for a padded look. Stick the self-adhesive ribbon down the long sides of the aperture using the embossed outline as a guide. For a professional finish, take a few stitches through the button holes in the little hearts before attaching them to the ends of the ribbon.

House Tag

The little house motif from page 40 of the More Card Ideas section uses the same colour palette as the jolly snail design. I've used a tag in fresh green with pale lilac checked paper to enhance the stitching. A twiggy heart echoes the one in the design, while the paper twine tie completes the country look.

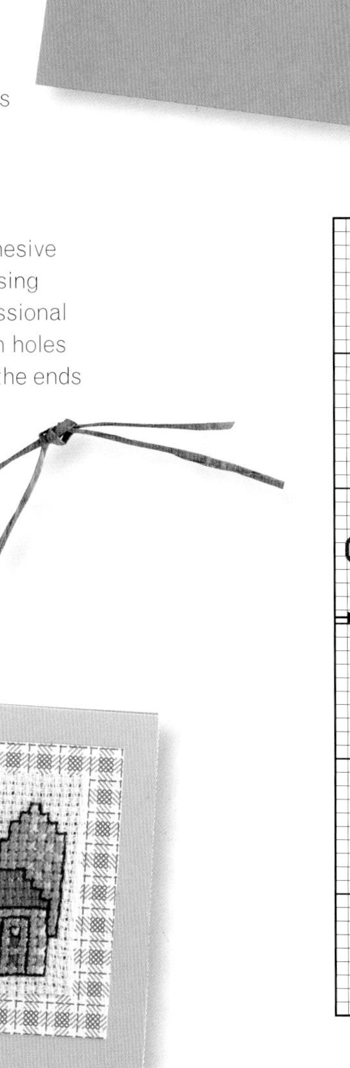

Tutu-tastic!

You will need

- 14-count silver perforated paper 7.6cm (3in) square
- DMC stranded cotton (floss) as listed in chart key
- Single-fold card 180 x 115mm (7 x 4½in) in pale pink
- Pink gingham patterned paper 11.5 x 8.5cm (4½ x 3¼in)
- Spatter-foam mesh, four rectangles each 9.5 x 3.5cm (3¾ x 1⅜in) in pink
- Small flower gem in pale pink
- Selection of ballet-themed charms/embellishments
- Scissors with decorative edging

Stitch count 28h x 26w
Design size 5 x 4.7cm (2 x 1⅞in)

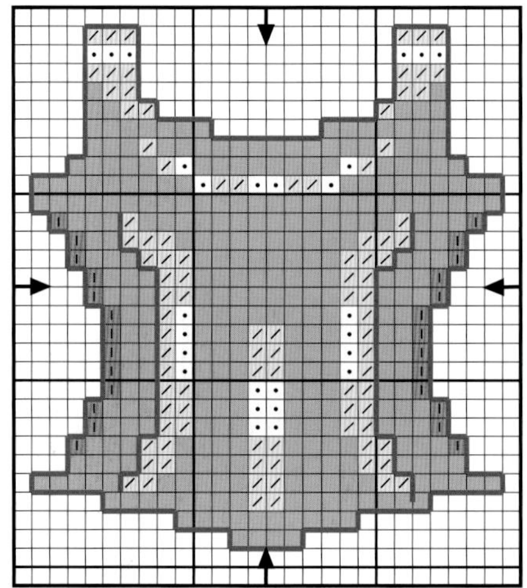

DMC stranded cotton
Cross stitch (2 strands)

- 603
- 604
- 605
- blanc

Backstitch (1 strand)

- 961

Note Stitch the design over one square of the perforated paper.

To craft the card Trim the finished stitching leaving one square all around the edge. To make the skirt of the tutu take the rectangles of pink spatter foam mesh and trim to shape the sides up to the stitched bodice and give a scalloped effect to the lower edge. Place some glue dots along the top edge of one of the pieces of mesh, and then layer the other pieces on top, pressing down firmly. Match up the skirt and bodice, securing with more glue dots. Add a pink flower gem to the bodice. Use decorative scissors to cut the long edges of the pink gingham paper. Attach to the card using double-sided tape and leaving a 1cm (⅜in) margin on the right-hand edge. Add the tutu using more tape, with the skirt slightly overlapping the gingham paper. To make this an extra special card for a little ballerina, use glue dots to add a selection of ballet-themed charms.

Make It Special

You could change this design into a gorgeous prom dress by adding a longer fabric skirt in a deeper colour and changing the card from a wide to a tall format – perfect for an 18th birthday card.

This card is perfect for a little girl's birthday. Use it for a ballet lover or substitute a golden crown and gemstones for a princess.

XXX

This would be a lovely keepsake to accompany a gift for a young bridesmaid. Use the colours of her dress and embellish with tiny padded hearts, ribbon roses and bows.

Wise Owl

You will need

14-count cream Aida 15cm (6in) square

DMC stranded cotton (floss) as listed in chart key

Double-fold card 155 x 110mm (6 x 4½in) with 90mm (3½in) rounded diamond aperture in gold linen effect

Wadding (batting) same size as finished design

Small piece of paper and red card

Gold stars and gold pen (optional)

Stitch count 39h x 40w
Design size 7 x 7.2cm (2¾ x 2⅞in)

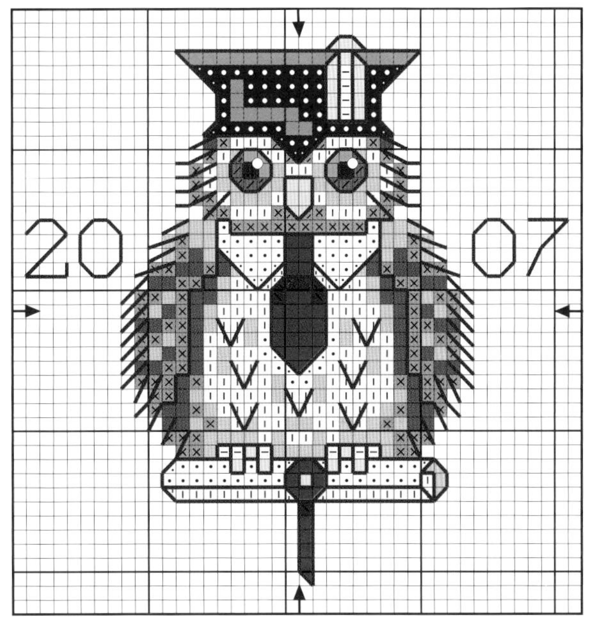

DMC stranded cotton
Cross stitch (2 strands)

310	435	666	725	838
414	437	720	727	blanc
434	498	722	739	

Backstitch (1 strand)
838

French knots (1 strand)
blanc

Note To change the date, use the numbers charted on page 23.

To craft the card Mount the finished stitching in the double-fold card (see page 8) using the wadding for a padded look. I made a scroll from a small piece of paper and used coloured pencils to shade it to look like vellum. A tiny scrap of red card cut to shape makes a seal. Add some gold stars and a message in gold pen. Use glue dots to stick the embellishments to the card.

Make It Special

If you don't like drawing but have a computer, search for clip art relating to graduation. Alternatively, look for packs of themed embellishments – the kind used by scrapbookers.

All Set to Go

You will need

14-count pearl lustre Aida 18 x 7.6cm (7 x 3in)

DMC stranded cotton (floss) and Light Effects thread as listed in chart key

Double-fold card 210 x 70mm (8¼ x 2¾in) with triple aperture in black

Wadding (batting) same size as finished design

Thin white card about 4cm (1½in) square

Stitch count 72h x 16w
Design size 13 x 2.9cm (5⅛ x 1⅛in)

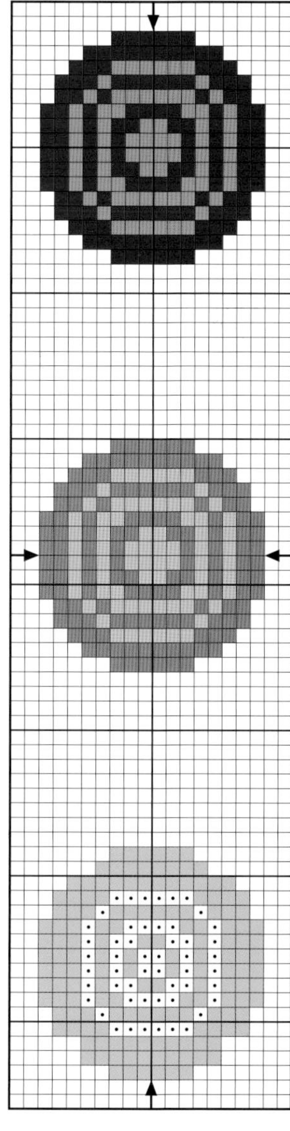

DMC stranded cotton
Cross stitch (2 strands)

- 352
- 666
- 741
- 970
- • blanc
- E990 Light Effects

Note Each aperture on this card measures 4cm (1½in) square. Use the measurements above if stitching the motifs on a single piece of Aida, leaving twelve squares between each light to fit into the spaces. Alternatively, stitch the motifs separately if you have fabric scraps to use up.

To craft the card Mount the finished stitching in the card (see page 8) using the wadding for a padded look. Use a red pencil to draw an L in the centre of the piece of white card. Cut the card in half with a zigzag effect and attach the two parts to the bottom of the card using a glue stick.

Make It Special

Using fluorescent green thread gives a fun touch to this card – not only does it give the appearance of the green light being at 'go' but it does actually glow in the dark too!

Car Card

This bright little card is great for any new driver. The motif, from page 43, can easily be stitched in an evening. Jelly letters form the greeting, which is offset on opposite edges of the aperture for a stylish look. I've added a red padded Lurex star as a finishing touch. Personalize the motif by changing the colour of the car or adding a registration number instead of the stitched words.

Pink Cadillac

You will need

14-count cream Aida 15 x 15cm (6 x 6in)

DMC stranded cotton (floss) as listed in chart key

Single-fold card 145mm (5¾in) square in bright pink

Iron-on adhesive

Thin card 3.5 x 11cm (1¼ x 4⅜in) in turquoise pearlescent (optional)

Your greeting – computer font (see page 9) or write your own, about 2.5 x 10cm (1 x 4in)

Silver die-cut key shape

Silver metallic thread about 8cm (3in)

Stitch count 50h x 50w
Design size 9cm (3½in) square

To craft the card Iron the adhesive on the back of the stitching (see page 7) and stick it to the pink card using double-sided tape. I used a computer font (Magneto 24pt) in bright pink to make my greeting, printing it out on glossy photo paper. If you don't have access to a computer, write your own message with a bright pink gel pen on some thin white card. Double up the metallic thread and loop it through the hole in the die-cut key. Cover the back of the turquoise card in double-sided tape and press one end of the silver thread to it before attaching the whole thing to the card front. The key should be left to swing free.

This would also be a great card to give to someone getting their first car – especially if they were lucky enough to be receiving it as a gift.

If you omitted the L-plate (stitching just white cross stitches in its place), this design could be used as a card for someone going on a long road trip.

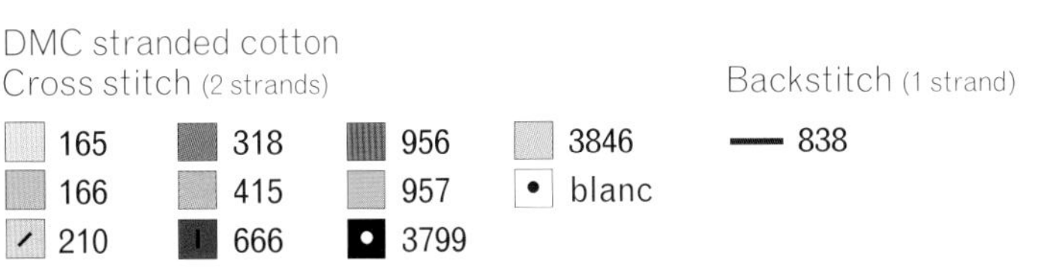

Anchors Away!

You will need

14-count cream Aida 15cm (6in) square

DMC stranded cotton (floss) as listed in chart key

Single-fold card 125mm (5in) square in pearlescent orange

Iron-on adhesive

Circle of silver holographic self-adhesive paper 9.5cm (3¾in) diameter

Stitch count 58h x 50w
Design size 10.5 x 9cm (4⅛ x 3½in)

To craft the card Iron the adhesive on to the back of the stitching (see page 7). Cut out the lettering and then the ship, leaving one square all around each motif. Stick the silver holographic circle to the card, leaving a larger margin at the bottom. Using more tape, centre and stick the ship motif to the circle and then attach the lettering below.

> You could stitch just the ship motif and mount it in a card with a circular aperture to give as a good luck card for someone emigrating.

DMC stranded cotton
Cross stitch (2 strands)

- 310
- 740
- 742
- 743
- 3041
- 3042
- 3740
- 3823
- blanc

Backstitch (1 strand)

- 310
- 3740

On Your Way!

You will need

28-count white evenweave 18 x 15cm (7 x 6in)

DMC stranded cotton (floss) as listed in chart key

Double-fold card 200 x 150mm (8 x 6in) with 145 x 95mm (5¾ x 3¾in) aperture in ivory

Wadding (batting) same size as finished design

Clear self-adhesive jelly letters for wording

Thin brown card about 4 x 7.6cm (1½ x 3in) for luggage tag (optional)

Thin paper twine or string 10cm (4in) (optional)

Stitch count 65h x 50w
Design size 11.8 x 9cm (4½ x 3½in)

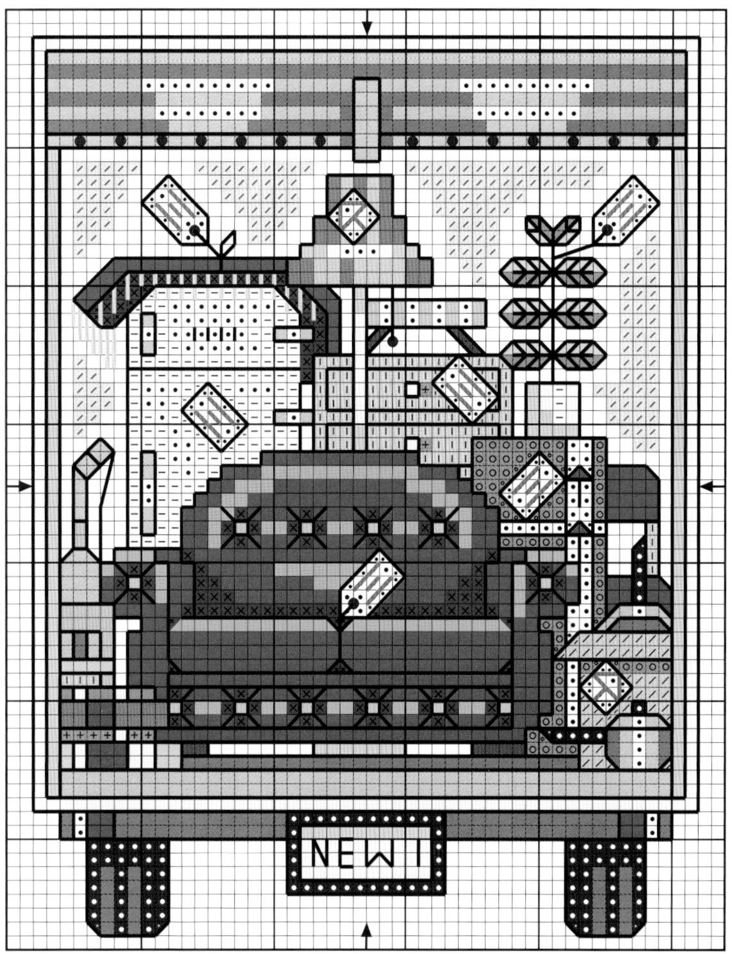

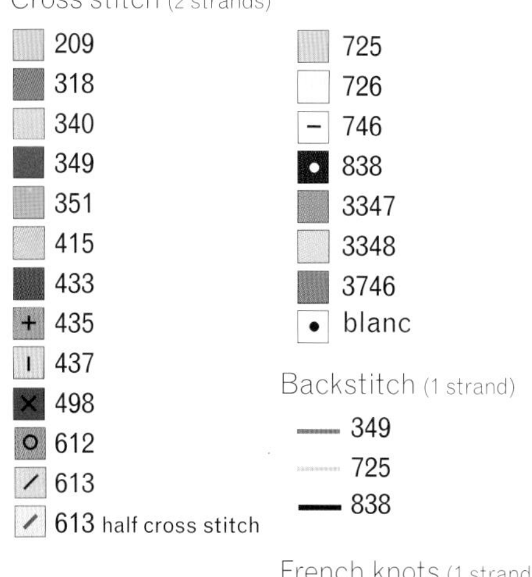

Note Remember to stitch over two threads of the evenweave fabric. There are some areas of the design stitched in half cross stitch (a single diagonal line) – use two strands of DMC 613 (shown with a red symbol on the chart).

To craft the card

Mount the finished stitching in the card (see page 8) using the wadding for a padded look. If adding the luggage tag to the card, position the stitching 1.25cm (½in) from the top edge of the aperture. Write your words on the tag. Decide on your message and add the jelly letters to the card. Running the wording around the edge gives a quirky look.

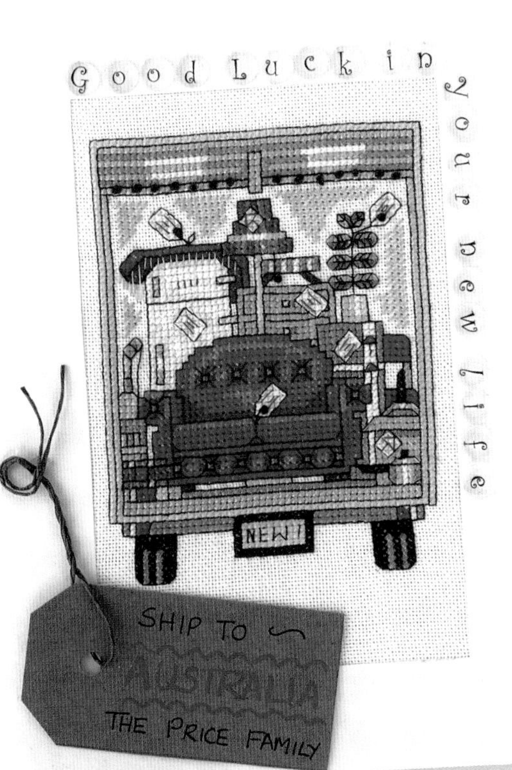

A New Baby
Girl
Welcome
Little
Darling

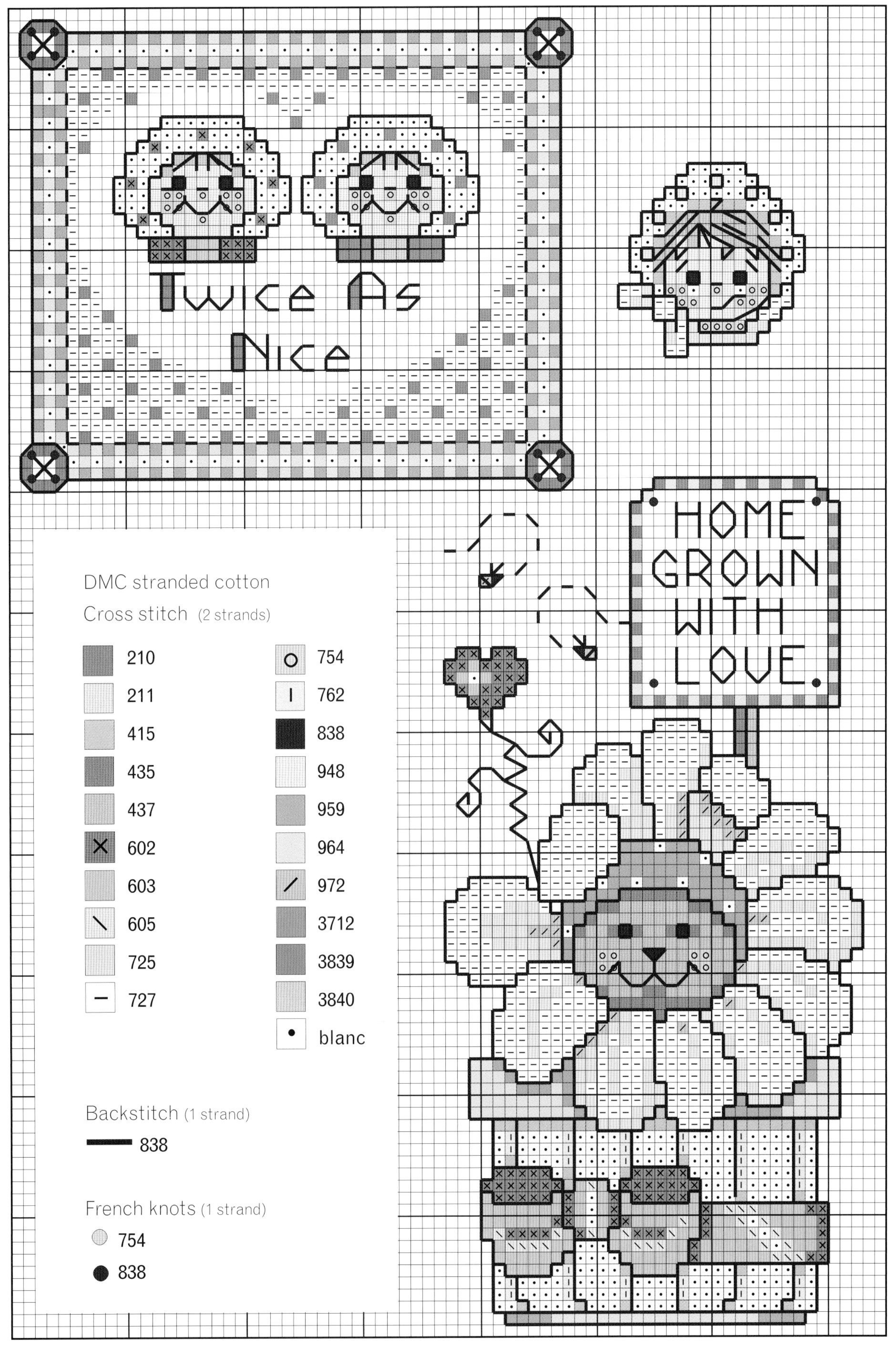

Twice As
Nice
HOME
GROWN
WITH
LOVE
DMC stranded cotton
Cross stitch (2 strands)
210
211
415
435
437
602
603
605
725
727
754
762
838
948
959
964
972
3712
3839
3840
blanc
Backstitch (1 strand)
838
French knots (1 strand)
754
838

With Love on your Wedding Day
With Love
GOOD LUCK!

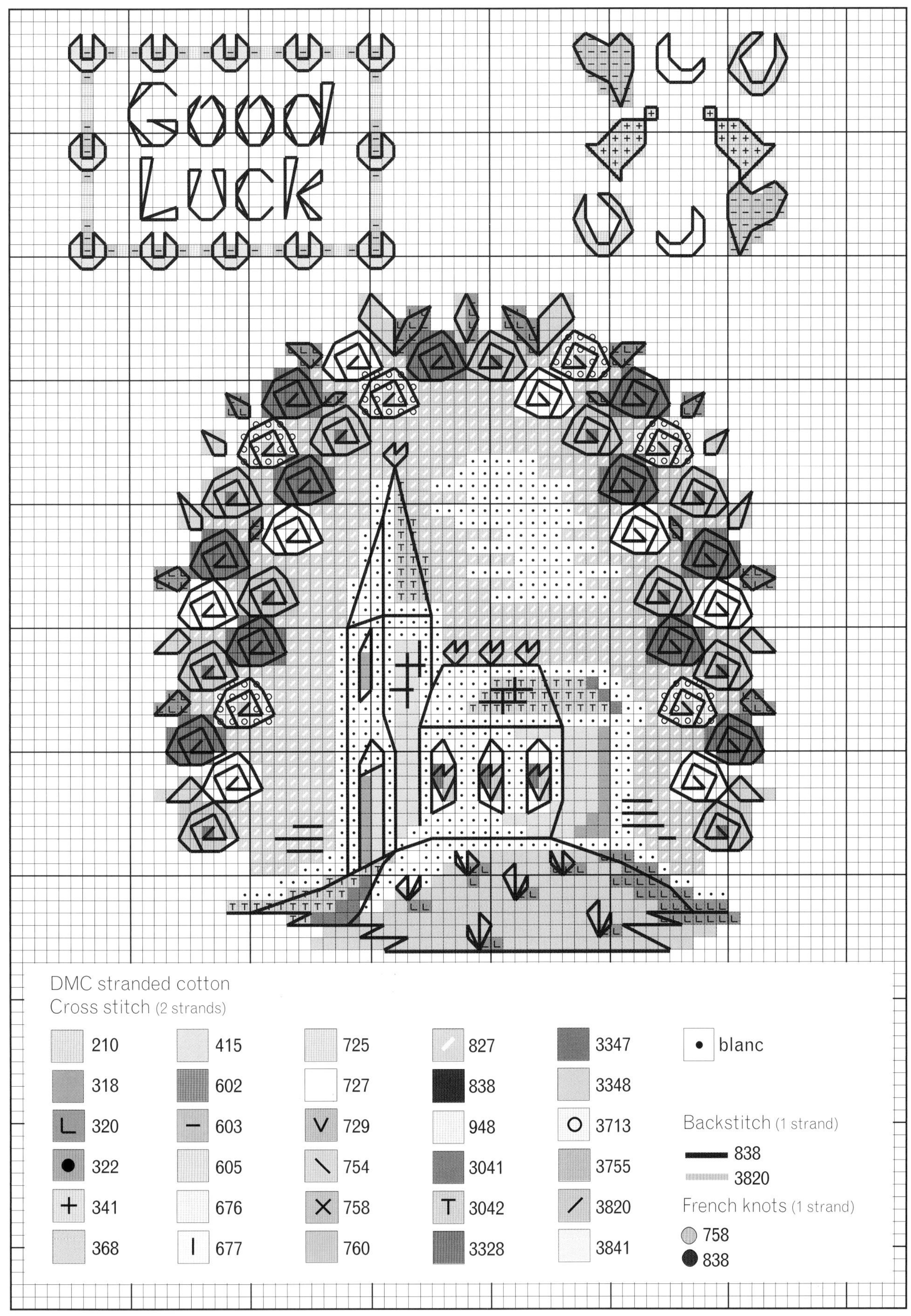
Good Luck
DMC stranded cotton
Cross stitch (2 strands)
210
318
L 320
● 322
+ 341
368
415
602
– 603
605
676
I 677
725
727
V 729
\ 754
X 758
760
827
838
948
3041
T 3042
3328
3347
3348
O 3713
3755
/ 3820
3841
• blanc
Backstitch (1 strand)
838
3820
French knots (1 strand)
758
838

30
40
Love
50
Evergreen
60
Precious
Years

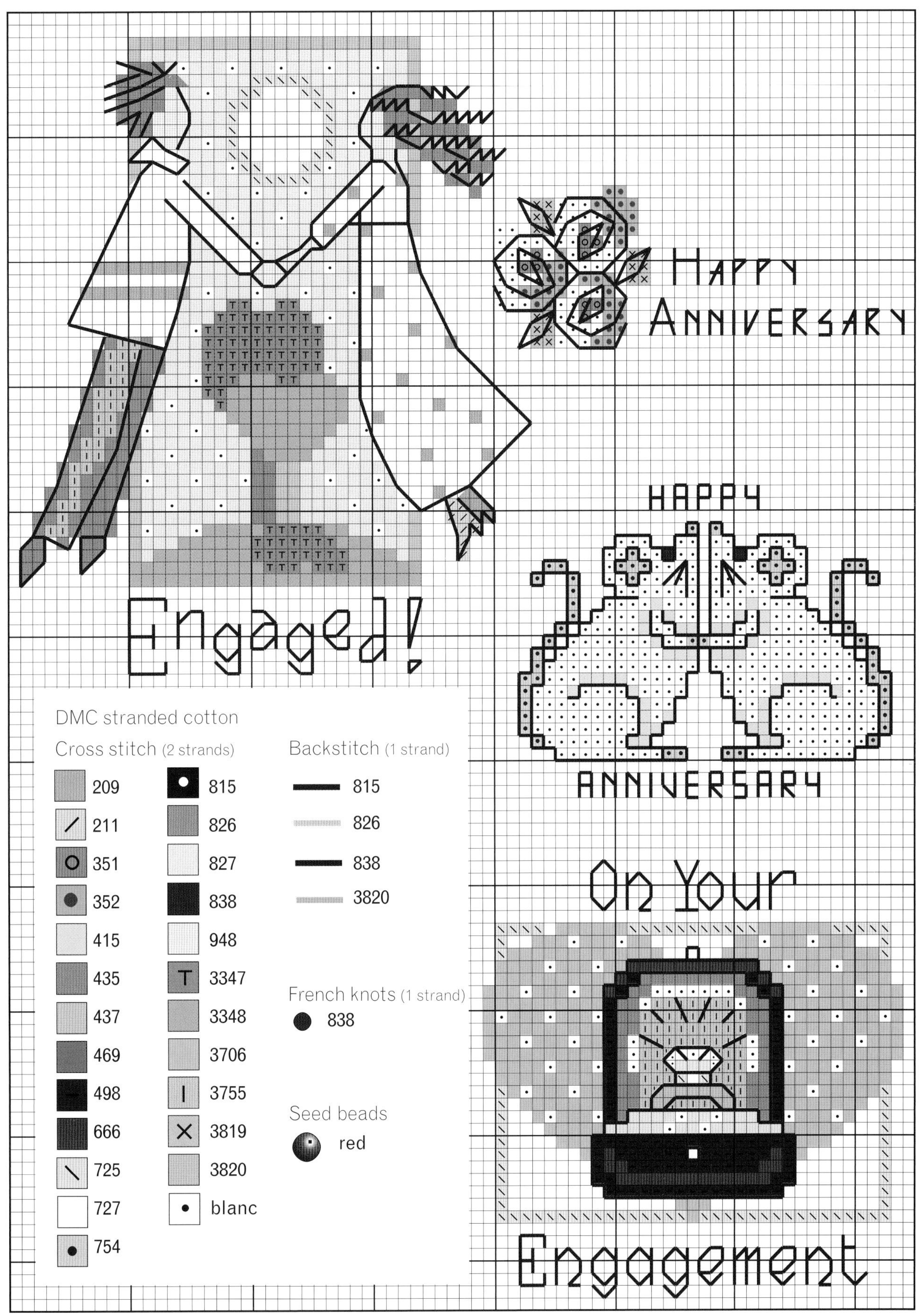
Engaged!
Happy Anniversary
Happy
Anniversary
On Your
Engagement
DMC stranded cotton
Cross stitch (2 strands)
209
211
351
352
415
435
437
469
498
666
725
727
754
815
826
827
838
948
3347
3348
3706
3755
3819
3820
blanc
Backstitch (1 strand)
815
826
838
3820
French knots (1 strand)
838
Seed beads
red

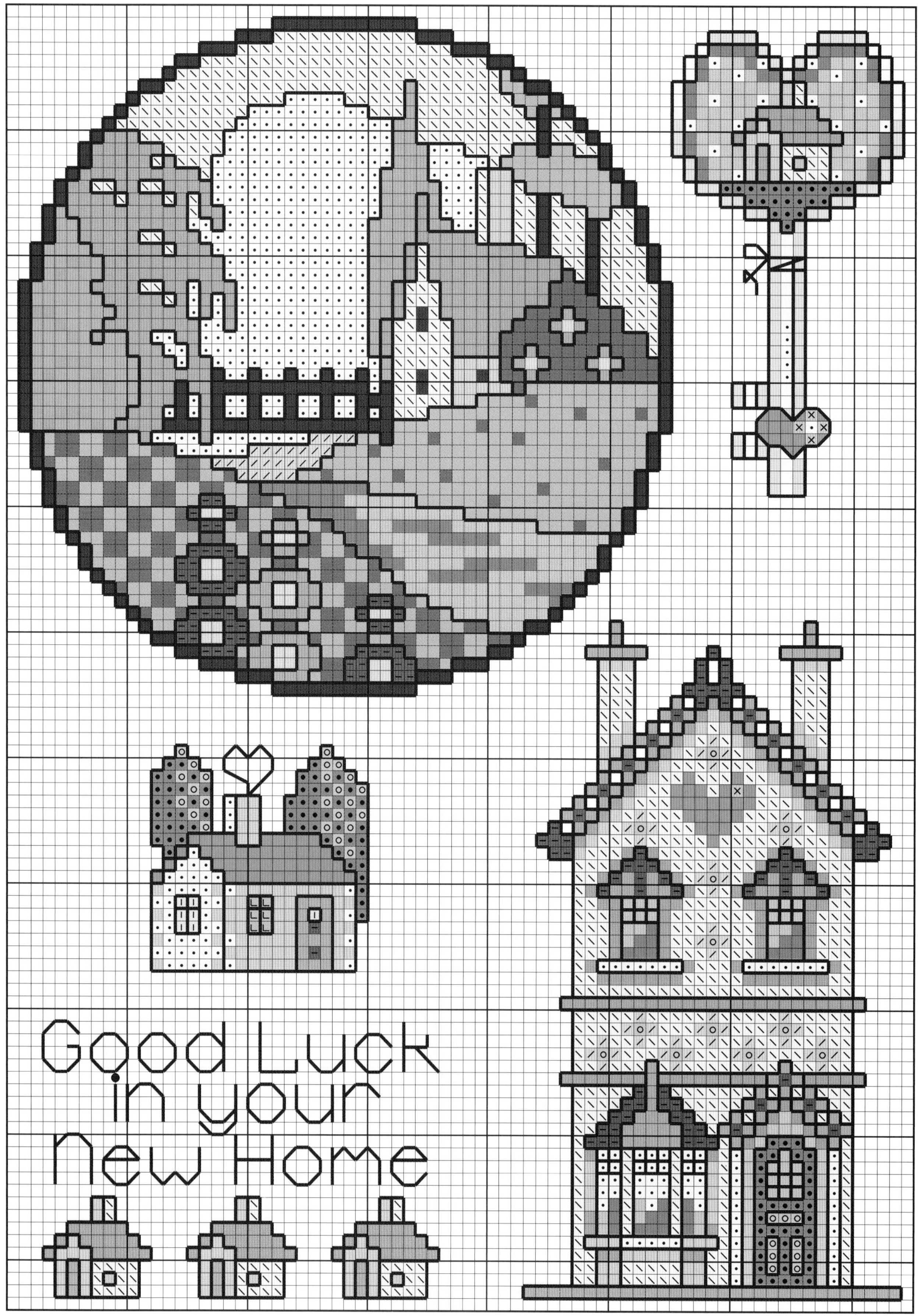
Good Luck
in your
New Home

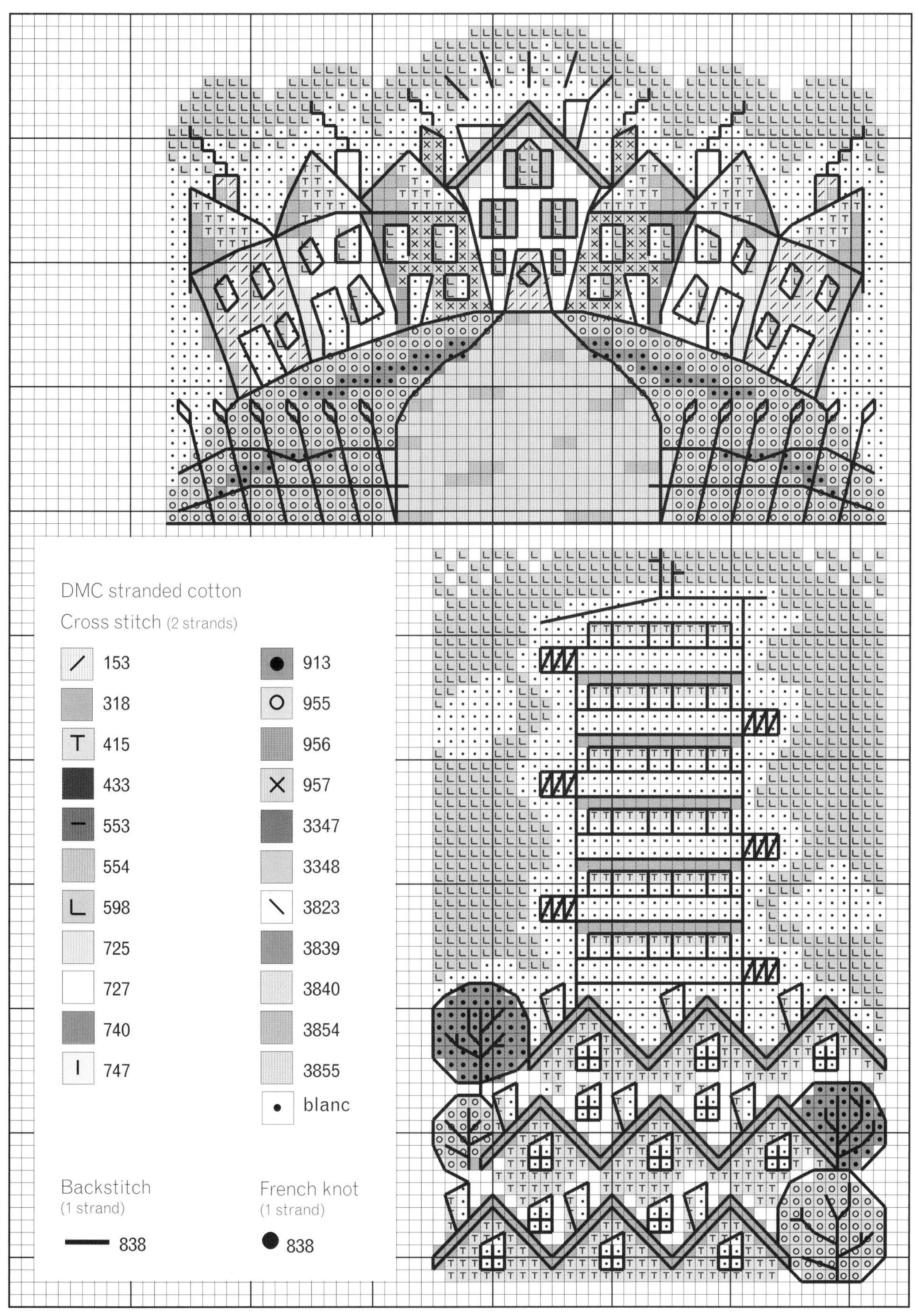
DMC stranded cotton
Cross stitch (2 strands)
153
318
415
433
553
554
598
725
727
740
747
913
955
956
957
3347
3348
3823
3839
3840
3854
3855
blanc
Backstitch
(1 strand)
838
French knot
(1 strand)
838

Congratulations
you made the
Grade!!!
Just A
Note To
Say
Well
Done!
Sorry you're
Leaving
WELL
DONE
THE FAT LADY
SINGS

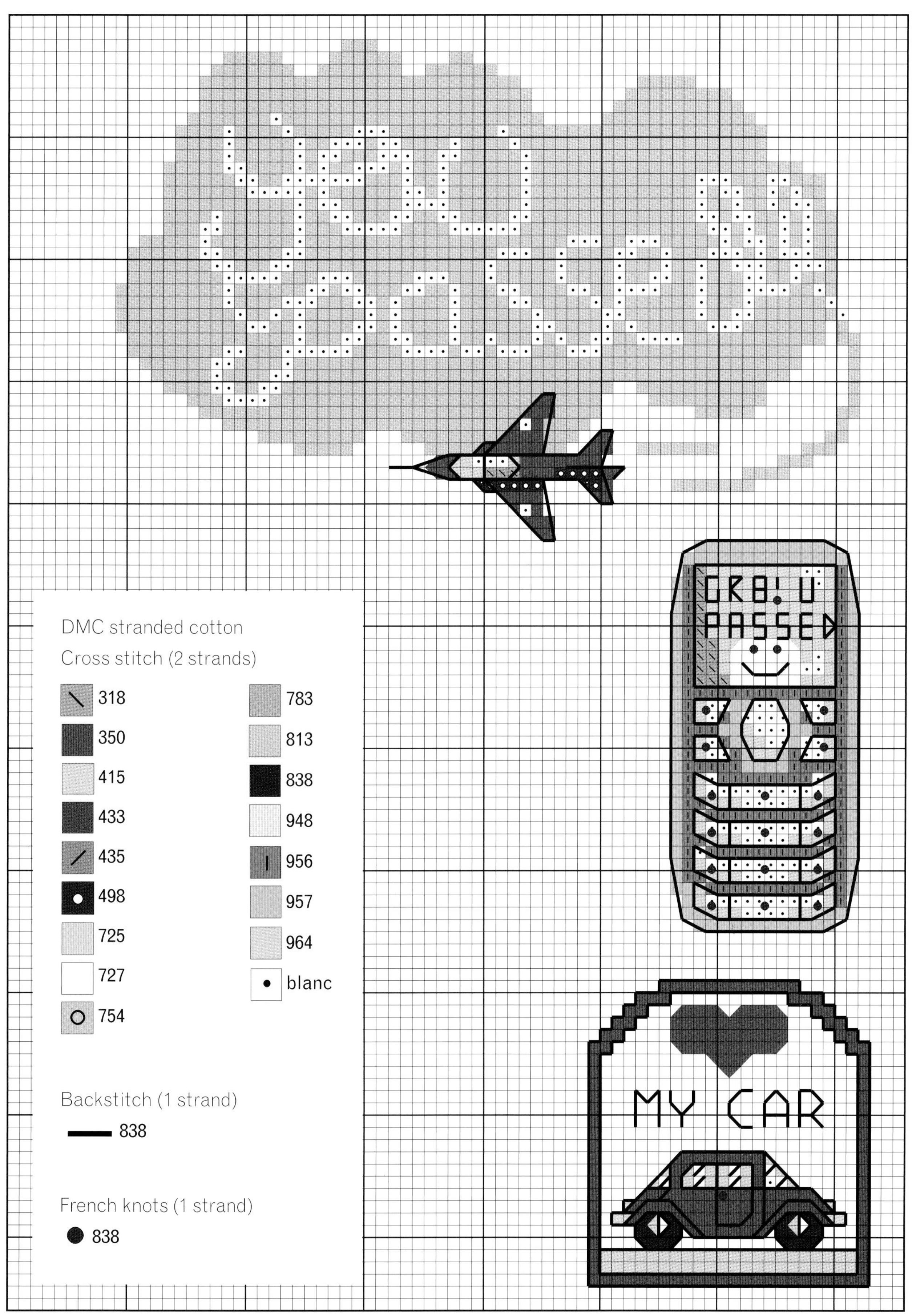

GR8! U PASSED
MY CAR
DMC stranded cotton
Cross stitch (2 strands)
318
350
415
433
435
498
725
727
754
783
813
838
948
956
957
964
blanc
Backstitch (1 strand)
838
French knots (1 strand)
838

Birthday Bonanza

As the chapter title suggests, you'll find a wealth of birthday designs here perfect for family and friends. Everything is included – from a first to a fiftieth and beyond, with all the milestone birthdays in between. A heart-shaped keepsake for a baby's first birthday features a sweet design with delicate colours and embellishments. Little girls will be thrilled to receive a lovely fairy wishes pin whilst older ones will cherish a friendship book in zingy colours or a pretty felt gift bag.

Fun cards for toddlers, younger children and teenagers all feature unusual but easy making-up techniques you'll want to try. For women you will find a gorgeous girly card and also one that's sure to make a shoe-lover smile. To ensure that the men are not overlooked you'll find projects for them too, including a noble knight made up into a handsome card with a matching gift tag. Eighteenth and thirtieth birthdays are celebrated in style, whilst those in their forties and fifties will enjoy two nostalgic designs. And why not award a green-fingered gardener or super cross stitcher with a World's Greatest card that's bound to be appreciated.

You'll find more brilliant birthday motifs to inspire you in More Card Ideas on pages 68–77.

5
Today!
CHIC
Have a
GORGEOUS
DAY!
Birthday
Princess
CH
CHEERS!

Precious Heart Keepsake

You will need

14-count white pearl-lustre Aida 23cm (9in) square

DMC stranded cotton (floss) as listed in chart key

Cardboard heart with holes for hanging 22.5 x 20cm (8¾ x 8in) x 1.25cm (½in) deep (see Suppliers)

White water-based paint and a medium paintbrush

Iron-on adhesive

Felt 25.5cm (10in) square in baby pink

White scalloped-edge lace 70cm (27½in) long x 1.25cm (½in) wide

Ribbon 41cm (16in) long x 6mm (¼in) wide in rose pink with gold edging

Organza ribbon 46cm (18in) x 2cm (¾in) wide in palest pink

Piece of card 5cm (2in) square in pale pink

Piece of thin craft foam 5cm (2in) square in deep pink

Small flower punch 2.5cm (1in)

Six pink and pearl flower embellishments

Four 2mm (⅛in) self-adhesive diamantes (optional)

Stitch count 80h x 70w
Design size 14.5 x 12.7cm (5¾ x 5in)

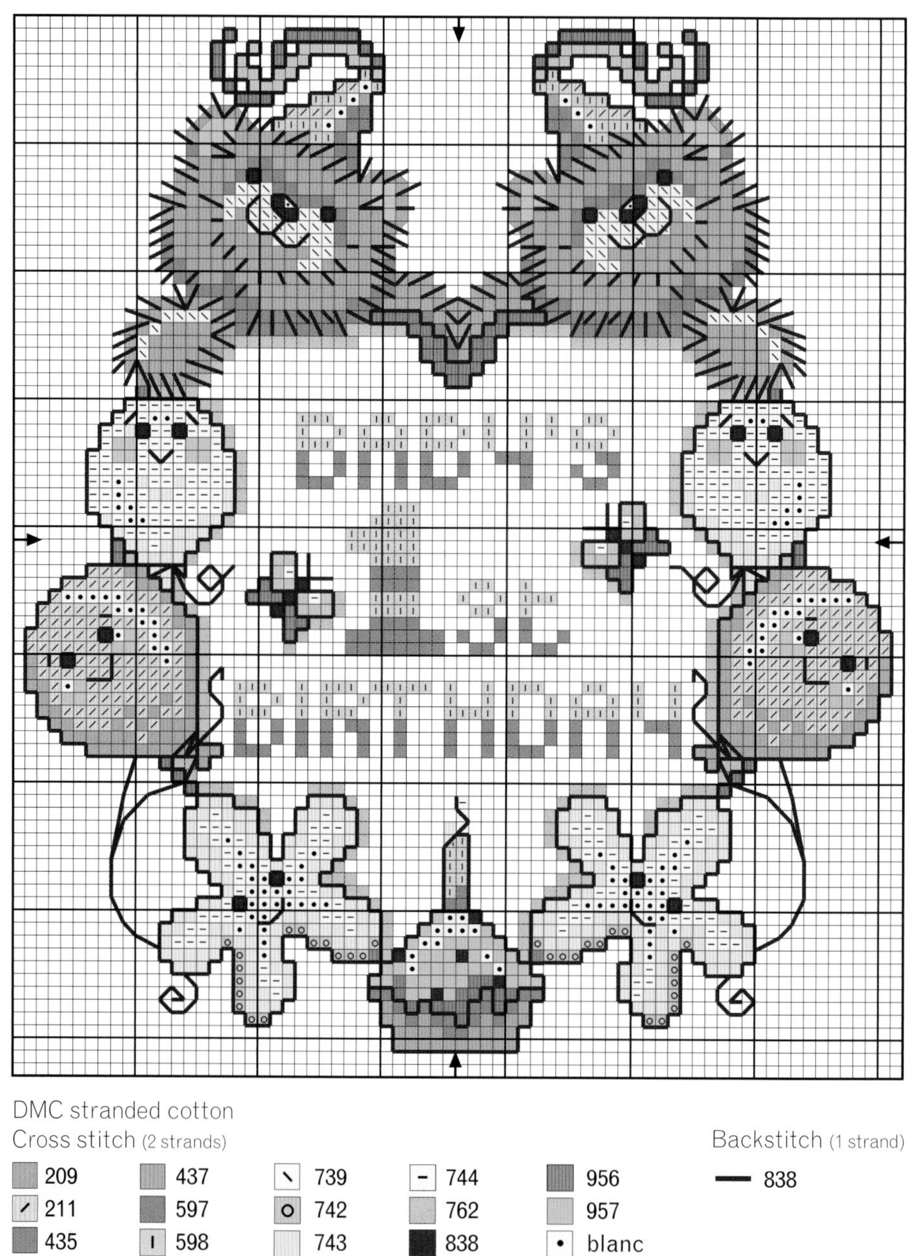

To craft the card Paint the heart, allowing each coat to dry. Trace the heart shape on to the felt. Use PVA glue to stick the felt on one side of the heart. Back the stitching with adhesive (see page 7) and cut out around the design leaving some Aida showing. Attach the stitching to the felt with double-sided tape. Mark the hanging holes with a darning needle. Beginning at the bottom, attach the lace around the heart's edge using double-sided tape. Punch out two flowers in pale pink card and two in thin craft foam. Needle pierce the centre of each flower. Stick two diamantes on each flower. Thread the needle with rose pink ribbon, knot one end and pass the needle through one hole to the front. Thread a deep pink and pale pink flower on to the ribbon to move them down to cover the hole. Feed on two more flowers and then pass the ribbon through the other hole, through to the back to form a hanging loop. With the heart hanging straight, stick down the knot at the back. Make an organza ribbon bow and stitch in place at the bottom. Fix a flower embellishment in the middle with a glue dot. Fix on the remaining flowers to finish.

Make It Special

Make the design suitable for a boy by using blue felt and self-adhesive blue gingham instead of lace. Replace flowers and ribbons with charms on a baby boy theme.

Baby's First Birthday

The fluffy teddy and butterflies from the heart keepsake appear on this little card (chart on page 74). Cut out the stitched motif and attach it to a champagne-coloured glitter card. Add a strip of self-adhesive ribbon and some pretty streamer embellishments to finish.

Two Today

You will need

14-count white Lurex Aida 15cm (6in) square

DMC stranded cotton (floss) as listed in chart key

Double-fold card with oval aperture 115 x 180mm (4½ x 7in) in pale blue cloud effect

Wadding (batting) same size as finished design

Three streamer embellishments in yellow, pink and turquoise (optional)

Mini glue dots

Stitch count 44h x 30w
Design size 8 x 5.5cm (3⅛ x 2⅛in)

To craft the card Mount the finished stitching in the card (see page 8) using wadding for a padded look. Use mini glue dots to stick the streamer embellishments on the card.

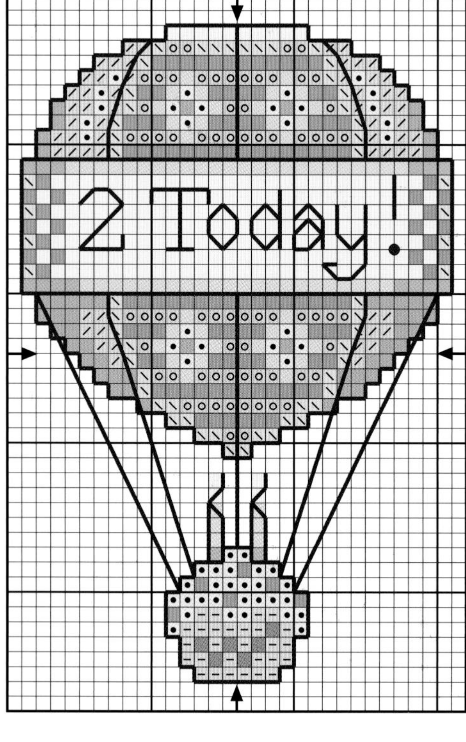

DMC stranded cotton
Cross stitch (2 strands)

- 209
- 211
- 435
- 437
- 725
- 727
- 956
- 957
- 959
- 964
- blanc

Backstitch (1 strand)

- 838

French knot (1 strand)

- 838

To stitch this for a 1st birthday, simply omit one of the candles and change the number on the balloon. You'll find more numbers in the alphabet section (see page 103). Look out for all the lovely embellishments available on a nursery theme.

This would also make a lovely tag for a special gift, such as a teddy. Iron some adhesive on to the back of the stitching (see page 7). Cut out around the curve of the balloon, but don't try cutting between the balloon ropes! Cut a piece of card slightly larger than the design and punch a hole at the top. Stick on the design using mini glue dots and thread some pretty ribbon through the tag.

Circus Clown

You will need

14-count cream Aida 10cm (4in) square

DMC stranded cotton (floss) as listed in chart key

Single-fold card 145mm (5¾in) square in pale lemon

Two strips of multicoloured stripe decorative paper each 14.5 x 5.5cm (5¾ x 2⅛in)

Self-adhesive ribbon 23cm (9in) long x 6mm (¼in) wide in sunflower yellow

Two pink swirl embellishments or similar

Iron-on adhesive

Self-adhesive letters in multicoloured metallic

Stitch count 40h x 31w
Design size 7.3 x 5.6cm (2⅝ x 2¼in)

To craft the card On the wrong side on each paper strip mark 5.5cm (2⅛in) down and 3cm (1⅛in) across. Draw a curved shaped to where the marks meet. Draw a straight line to the bottom. Cut out and stick the 'curtains' to the card front using double-sided tape. Cut self-adhesive ribbon 15.5cm (6in) long and stick to the top edge, folding the ends to the sides. Cut the remaining ribbon in half and stick at an angle for tie-backs. Fix the swirl embellishments with mini glue dots. Iron the adhesive on the back of the stitching (see page 7) and cut out leaving a square all round. Fix in place with mini glue dots. Arrange the lettering as shown or handwrite your own greeting. Numbers 1 to 7, each with a different clown motif, are charted on pages 68–69.

Make It Special

Make your card special by using real fabric (backed with iron-on adhesive to stop fraying) or felt to make your curtains. Or make your own decorative paper using coloured pencils. Textured paper works best for this, giving the same effect as my stripy curtains.

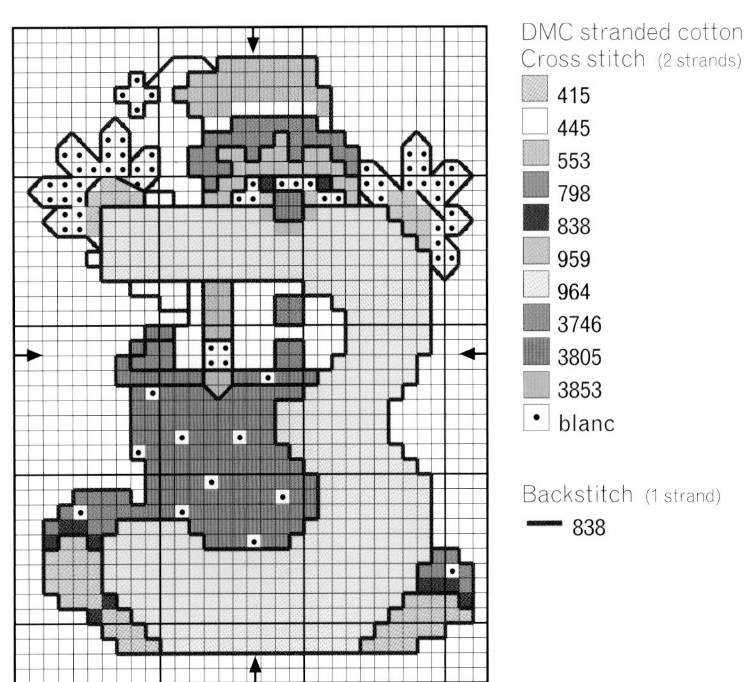

DMC stranded cotton
Cross stitch (2 strands)

- 415
- 445
- 553
- 798
- 838
- 959
- 964
- 3746
- 3805
- 3853
- • blanc

Backstitch (1 strand)

- 838

Fairy Wishes

You will need

28-count white evenweave 10cm (4in) square

DMC stranded cotton (floss) as listed in chart key

Iron-on adhesive

Card circle 7cm (2¾in) diameter in white

Card circle 5cm (2in) diameter in pearlescent pale pink

Ribbon 1m long x 2.5cm (1in) wide in pale pink/rainbow lustre effect

Organza ribbon 41cm (16in) long x 9cm (3½in) wide in pale pink

Wired furry chenille stem 21cm (8¼in) in pink/rainbow lustre effect

Eight self-adhesive 6mm (¼in) diamantes in pale pink

Two pink and pearl flower embellishments

Self-adhesive brooch back with safety catch 6mm x 4cm (¼ x 1½in) (see Suppliers)

Stitch count 40h x 40w
Design size 7.3cm (2⅞in) diameter

Note Remember to stitch over two threads of the evenweave fabric.

To craft the card Iron the adhesive on to the back of the stitching (see page 7). Cut out, leaving two threads all round. Stick to the white card circle with double-sided tape. Use a glue dot to fix one end of the ribbon to the bottom back of the card. Form a rosette by looping 2.5cm (1in) of ribbon and fixing to the card with a glue dot. Repeat all the way round, then trim the ribbon. Make a large bow from organza ribbon, secure using a needle and thread and pull tight in the centre. Wrap the chenille stem around the bow several times. Curl the ends up and add the flower embellishments with glue dots. Fix the bow off centre to the lower edge and stick diamantes on the rosette ribbons. Use double-sided tape to stick the pearlescent circle on the back and add the brooch back. Numbers 1 to 9 are charted on page 70.

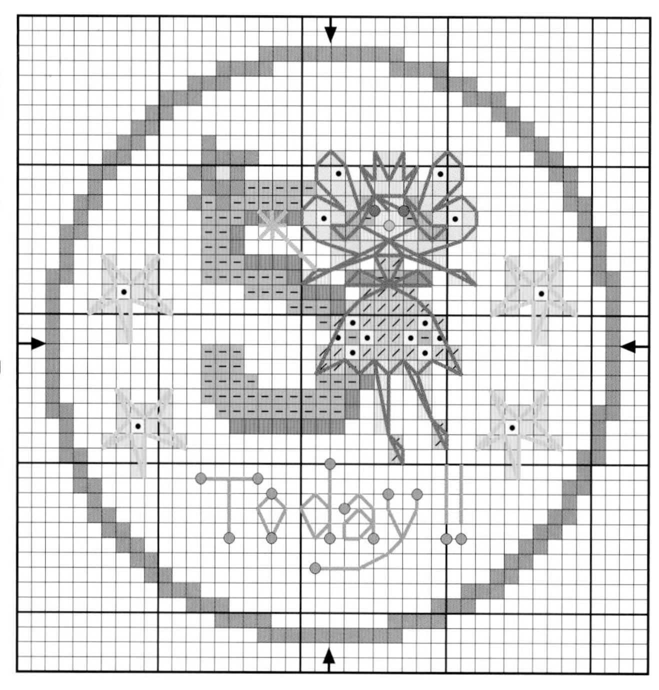

DMC stranded cotton
Cross stitch (2 strands)

- 209
- 211
- 437
- 603
- 605
- 727
- 747
- 754
- 964
- blanc

Backstitch (1 strand)

- 209 (1 strand)
- 728 (2 strands)
- 3041 (1 strand)
- 5283 silver metallic (1 strand)

French knots (1 strand)

- 209
- 605
- 3041

Cutie-Pie Cake

You will need

14-count cream Aida 13cm (5in) square

DMC stranded cotton (floss) as listed in chart key

Double-fold card 155 x 110mm (6 x 4½in) with rounded diamond aperture 90mm (3½in) in sunflower yellow

Wadding (batting) same size as finished card

Die-cut oval 4 x 6cm (1½ x 2¼in) in bright pink

Self-adhesive ribbon about 10cm (4in) long x 6mm (¼in) wide in pale pink

Happy Birthday rub-on or peel-off in silver to fit oval

Small amount of decorative card in pale pink polka dot and thin craft foam in deep pink (optional)

Small flower punch and single hole punch

Stitch count 32h x 32w
Design size 5.8cm (2¼in) square

To craft the card Mount the stitching in the card (see page 8) using wadding for a padded look. Punch a hole either side of the die-cut oval. Cut the ribbon in half and put a piece through each hole, folding to the back. Centre the oval below the aperture with the ribbon straight and taut. Stick the ribbon down, folding ends to the back. Add a Happy Birthday rub-on to the oval. Use the flower punch on the polka dot card and the thin craft foam. Punch a single hole out of craft foam for the polka dot flower centre. Fix to one side of the oval with glue dots.

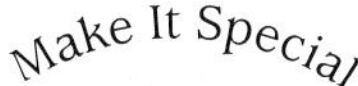

Make It Special

This design would make a great birthday cake band. Stitch the motif on 7.6cm (3in) wide Aida band, long enough to go around your cake, repeating the motif as necessary.

DMC stranded cotton
Cross stitch (2 strands)

209, 211, 725, 727, 762, 838, 956, 957, 959, 964, blanc

Backstitch (1 strand)

838

Birthday Princess

You will need

14-count cream Aida 18cm (7in) square

DMC stranded cotton (floss) as listed in chart key, plus 51cm (20in) of 676 and 25.5cm (10in) of 729 for plaits

Single-fold card 105 x 210mm (4 x 8¼in) in 'Fairy' (pale pink) cord texture

Iron-on adhesive

Piece of card 8 x 21cm (3⅛ x 8¼in) in 'Elf' (pale green) cord texture

Piece of card 1.25 x 5.5cm (½ x 2⅛in) in pale lilac, plus scraps for punching (optional)

Small fleur-de-lys punch (optional)

Two small fabric daisies 6mm (¼in) in white

Stitch count 64h x 23w
Design size 11.3 x 4.2cm (4½ x 1¾in)

Note Use the measurements above if stitching the motifs on a single piece of Aida or stitch them separately if you have fabric scraps to use up.

To craft the card Iron the adhesive on the back of the stitching (see page 7). Cut out the motifs leaving a square all round. Cut the 676 thread into four equal lengths and the 729 in half and mix up. Thread a needle with six strands, knot the end and bring to the front of the stitching at the collar. Repeat twice more. Repeat for the other side then plait and secure the strands leaving a little at the bottom. Add a white daisy on each with a mini glue dot. On the wrong side of the green card mark 11.5cm (4½in) up from the bottom. Mark the centre point and draw a rectangle 4.5cm (1¾in) high x 4cm (1½in) wide. Mark the centre point 2.5cm (1in) above the top of the rectangle. Draw up from the sides of the rectangle to the centre point, forming a pointed arch. Draw a line 1.25cm (½in) down from the top edge and mark at 1.25cm (½in) intervals. Rule them off vertically to make the castellated effect. Using a craft knife and metal ruler cut out the window and castellation. On the right side of the card, stick the strip of lilac card below the window. Using double-sided tape, stick the tower on the pink card. Using mini glue dots stick the princess into the window, as shown. Stick the banner below. Punch six fleur-de-lys from lilac card and fix in the places shown.

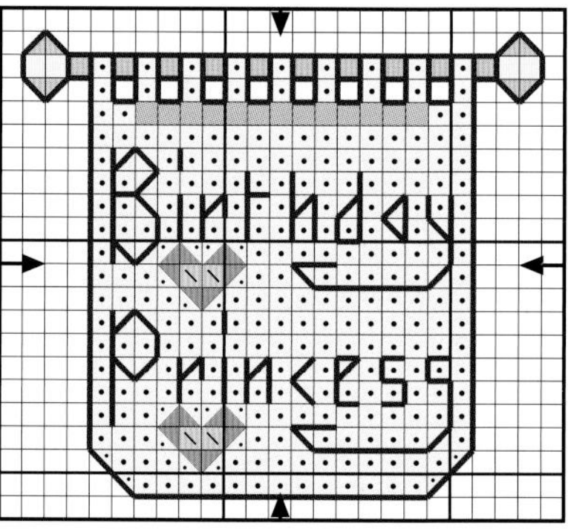

DMC stranded cotton
Cross stitch (2 strands)

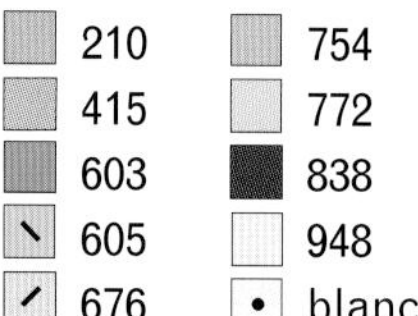

210	754	727 + E3821 Light Effects (1 strand of each)
415	772	
603	838	
605	948	3820 + E3821 Light Effects (1 strand of each)
676	blanc	
729		

Backstitch (1 strand)
— 838

Skater Boy

You will need

14-count cream Aida 23cm (9in) square

DMC stranded cotton (floss) as listed in chart key

Single-fold card 105 x 210mm (4⅛ x 8¼in) in bright orange

Iron-on adhesive

Decorative paper 10.5 x 21cm (4⅛ x 8¼in) in brick effect

Small foam pads

Stitch count 95h x 46w
Design size 17.2 x 8.3cm (6¾ x 3¼in)

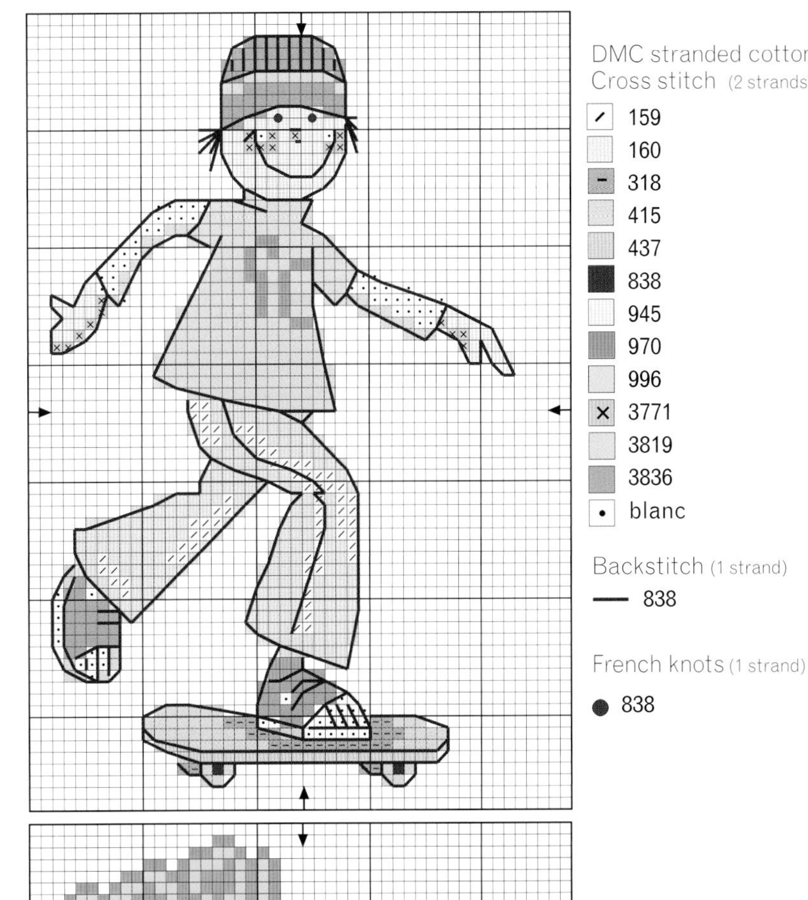

Note Stitch the motifs separately if you have fabric scraps to use up. A similar design for a girl skater can be found in More Card Ideas on page 74.

To craft the card Iron the adhesive on to the back of the stitching (see page 7). Cut out the skater and lettering, leaving a small amount of Aida all round. Attach the brick-effect paper to the front of the card with double-sided tape. Stick the skater to the card front with small foam pads – align the skateboard wheels with the lower edge of the card and his head protruding above the wall. Arrange the lettering like graffiti and fix with mini glue dots.

Friends Forever

You will need

14-count cream Aida 15cm (6in) square

DMC stranded cotton (floss) as listed in chart key

Spiral-bound notebook 14 x 12cm (5½ x 4¾in) in bright pink

Iron-on adhesive

Decorative card 9cm (3½in) square in lime green polka dot, plus scrap for punching

Self-adhesive ribbon 16cm (6¼in) long x 6mm (¼in) wide in pink gingham

Flower embellishment in pink and pearl

Four 2mm (⅛in) self-adhesive diamantes in pink

Small flower punch

Suitable text (from scrapbooking paper)

Stitch count 41h x 41w
Design size 7.4cm (3in) square

To craft the card Iron the adhesive on to back of the stitching (see page 7). Cut out the motif leaving a small amount of Aida all round. Stick the gingham ribbon down the right edge of the cover, folding edges to the back. Use double-sided tape to stick the polka dot paper 6mm (¼in) from the top. Fix the motif on top with mini glue dots, adding diamantes to the corners. Add your text below. To finish, fix a coloured flower embellishment on top of a flower punched from polka dot paper.

Make It Special

Add a bookmark to the notebook as a pretty finishing touch. Cut a strip of clear acetate 2 x 13.5cm (¾ x 5⅜in) and punch a hole in the centre top. Add the word 'Friend' in some funky stick-on letters down the strip. Thread some narrow rose pink ribbon through the hole and tie the bookmark to the notebook, trimming the ribbon ends to finish.

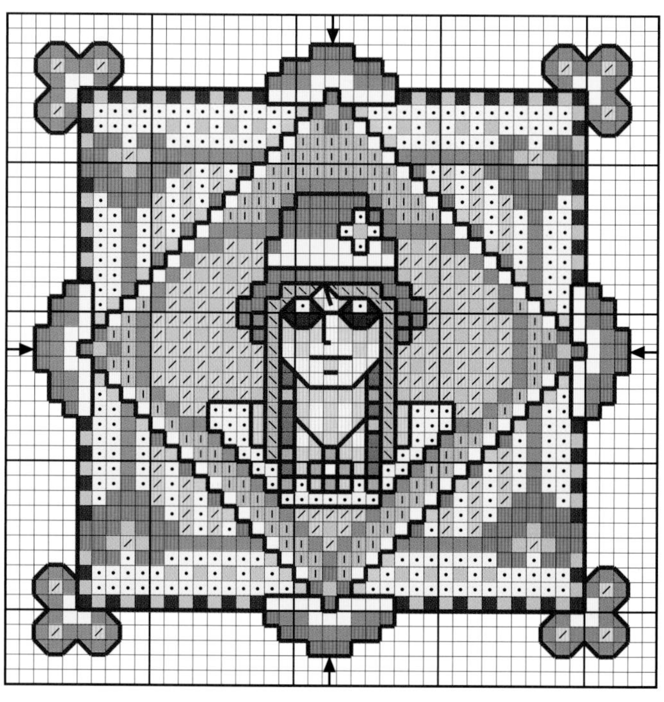

DMC stranded cotton
Cross stitch (2 strands)

209, 340, 415, 435, 437, 445, 602, 604, 754, 838, 948, 955, 3746, blanc

Backstitch (1 strand)

— 838

Cool Dude

You will need

28-count white evenweave 15cm (6in) square

DMC stranded cotton (floss) as listed in chart key

Single-fold card 148mm (5¾in) square in mid blue

Iron-on adhesive

Piece of card 4 x 14.8cm (1½ x 5¾in) in pearlescent mid blue

Decorative paper 14.8 x 16cm (5¾ x 6¼in) in snow effect

Used CD

Happy Birthday rub-on in silver

Stitch count 43h x 43w
Design size 7.8cm (3in) diameter

Note Remember to stitch over two threads of the evenweave fabric.

To craft the card Iron the adhesive on to the back of the stitching (see page 7). Cut out the motif leaving two threads all round. Fix the stitching to the CD with glue dots. Stick the decorative paper to the front of the card with double-sided tape, lining it up with the right edge and folding excess to the back. Use more tape to stick on the pearlescent card. Position the CD on the card front so it overlaps the strip of card and secure using tape. Finish off with the Happy Birthday rub-on.

This is a great card to accompany a gift of a music or games CD or DVD. If you don't have a spare CD substitute it with a circle of holographic self-adhesive paper 11.5cm (4½in) in diameter.

You could use the motif to make a card for a keen snowboarder by cutting out the decorative snow-effect paper to resemble mountain slopes and sticking it to a metallic blue card. Position the design above them and then add a rub-on greeting.

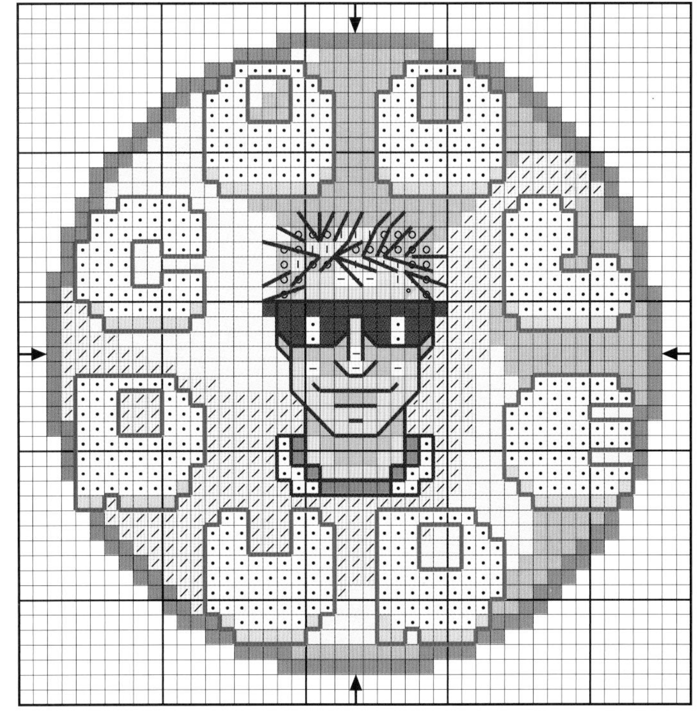

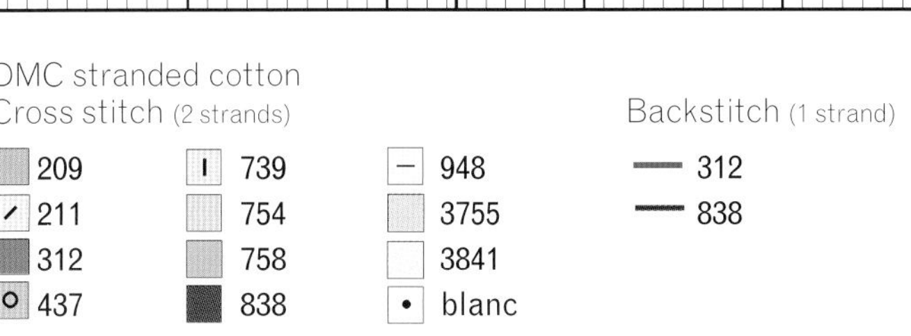

Cheers!

You will need

28-count white evenweave 13 x 12cm (5 x 4¾in)

DMC stranded cotton (floss) as listed in chart key

Single-fold card 100 x 145mm (4 x 5¾in) in 'Apple Fizz' glitter (see Suppliers)

Iron-on adhesive

Stitch count 58h x 41w
Design size 10.5 x 7.5cm (4⅛ x 3in)

Note Remember to stitch over two threads of the evenweave fabric.

To craft the card Iron the adhesive on the back of the stitching (see page 7). Cut out, following the design and leaving two or three threads of evenweave all round. Stick to the card using glue dots.

DMC stranded cotton
Cross stitch (2 strands)

• 165	996
613	3819
740	

Backstitch (1 strand)

- 740
- 838
- 996

Make It Special

This design would be great added to the cover of a photo album or scrapbook, tied up with satin ribbons – perfect to mark an 18th birthday occasion. See page 76 for a 21st birthday design.

Jeeves

You will need

28-count white evenweave 16 x 9cm (6¼ x 3½in)

DMC stranded cotton (floss) as listed in chart key

Single-fold card 100 x 210mm (4 x 8¼in) in ridged white

Iron-on adhesive

Piece of decorative card 6.5 x 12.5cm (2½ x 5in) in dark grey polka dot

Piece of decorative card 3 x 8cm (1⅛ x 3⅛in) in red pearlescent

Happy Birthday rub-on in silver

Small foam pads

Stitch count 57h x 27w
Design size 10.3 x 5 x 10cm (4 x 2in)

Note Remember to stitch over two threads of the evenweave fabric. There are some areas worked in half cross stitch (a single diagonal line) – use two strands of DMC 415 (shown with a red symbol on the chart).

To craft the card

Iron the adhesive on the back of the stitching (see page 7). Cut out following the shape of the design leaving two or three threads of evenweave all round. Stick the polka dot card 2.5cm (1in) below the top edge of the card with double-sided tape. Stick the stitched piece slightly off-centre on top of this with mini glue dots. Centre the greeting on the piece of red card and finish by attaching it to the card with small foam pads.

DMC stranded cotton
Cross stitch (2 strands)

- 317
- 415
- 415 half cross stitch
- 838
- 945
- 3801
- blanc

Backstitch (1 strand)

- 838

French knot (1 strand)

- 838

Noble Knight

You will need

28-count antique cream evenweave 15cm (6in) square

DMC stranded cotton (floss) as listed in chart key

Single-fold card 148mm (5¾in) square in 'Vine' (burgundy) cord texture

Iron-on adhesive

Piece of 'Essence Vintage' (pale gold) card 10.5 x 11cm (4 x 4½in) plus extra for punching

Piece of decorative paper 5 x 14.8cm (2 x 5¾in) in red/gold harlequin

Self-adhesive ribbon 15cm (6in) long x 6mm (¼in) wide in rich red

Small fleur-de-lys punch

Stitch count 52h x 47w
Design size 9.5 x 8.5cm (3¾ x 3⅜in)

Note Remember to stitch over two threads of the evenweave fabric.

DMC stranded cotton
Backstitch (1 strand)

— 830

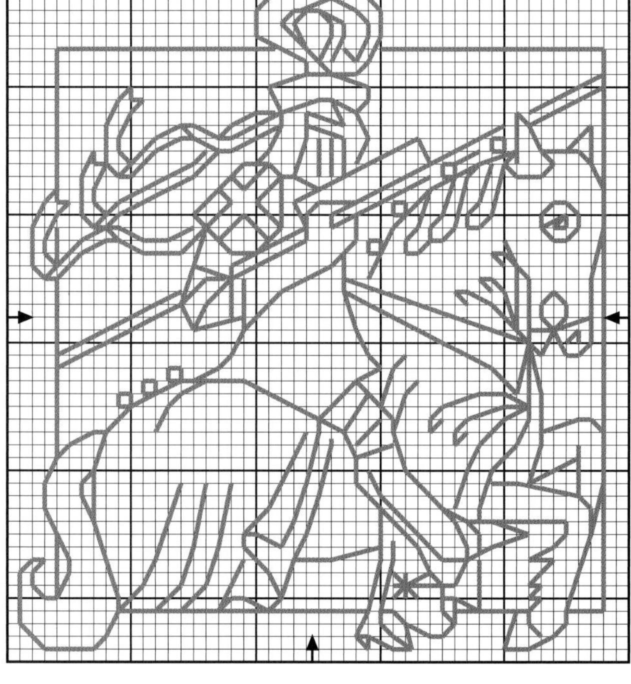

To craft the card

Iron adhesive on to the back of the stitching (see page 7). Cut out around the design leaving two threads all round. Lightly fold the harlequin paper in half and cover the wrong side with double-sided tape. Wrap it around the fold of the card. Cut the ribbon into three equal lengths. Fix a piece 2cm (¾in) below the top as shown, wrapping round to the back. Do the same with the other pieces, equally spaced. Punch three fleur-de-lys from gold card scraps and fix to the ends of the ribbon with glue dots. Fix the gold card to the front of the card with double-sided tape. Use mini glue dots to stick the stitching on top.

Heraldic Tag

Taking the theme of the card for inspiration, I made this rich-looking gift tag (chart on page 77), which could also be used as a bookmark. Cut out the shield and fix it to a rectangle of dull gold card, adding this to a stripe of decorative paper. Thread a gold twisted cord through a punched hole and add a fleur-de-lys to finish.

Gone Fishing

You will need

14-count cream Aida 18 x 13cm (7 x 5in)

DMC stranded cotton (floss) as listed in chart key

Single-fold card 145 x 210mm (5¾in x 8¼in) in pale grey marble effect

Piece of card 14.5 x 21cm (5¾ x 8¼in) in mid grey

Piece of clear acetate 11 x 14cm (4½ x 5½in)

Wood-effect alphabet tiles

Selection of embellishments (optional)

Stitch count 56h x 46w
Design size 10 x 8.3cm (4 x 3¼in)

To craft the card Draw a rectangle 9.5 x 12cm (3¾ x 4¾in) in the centre of the piece of mid-grey card. Cut out the aperture using a metal ruler and craft knife. Stick the acetate over the aperture with double-sided tape. Put the stitching on the acetate, right side down, and fix with tape. Put more tape around the edges of the grey card and attach it to the single-fold card. Add the greeting using wood-effect tiles. For an embellishment I used a ready-made paper tag, some leaf and acorn shapes and a fishing fly cut from scrapbook paper. Add paper twine tied in a knot and fix it all to the card with mini glue dots.

Make It Special

Unable to find a card with quite the right colour or size of aperture for this design, I created this simple custom version. Cutting apertures in this way avoids the need for making extra folds in the card to cover the back of your stitching. The combination of the shiny acetate and grey cards adds to the rainy effect of the design.

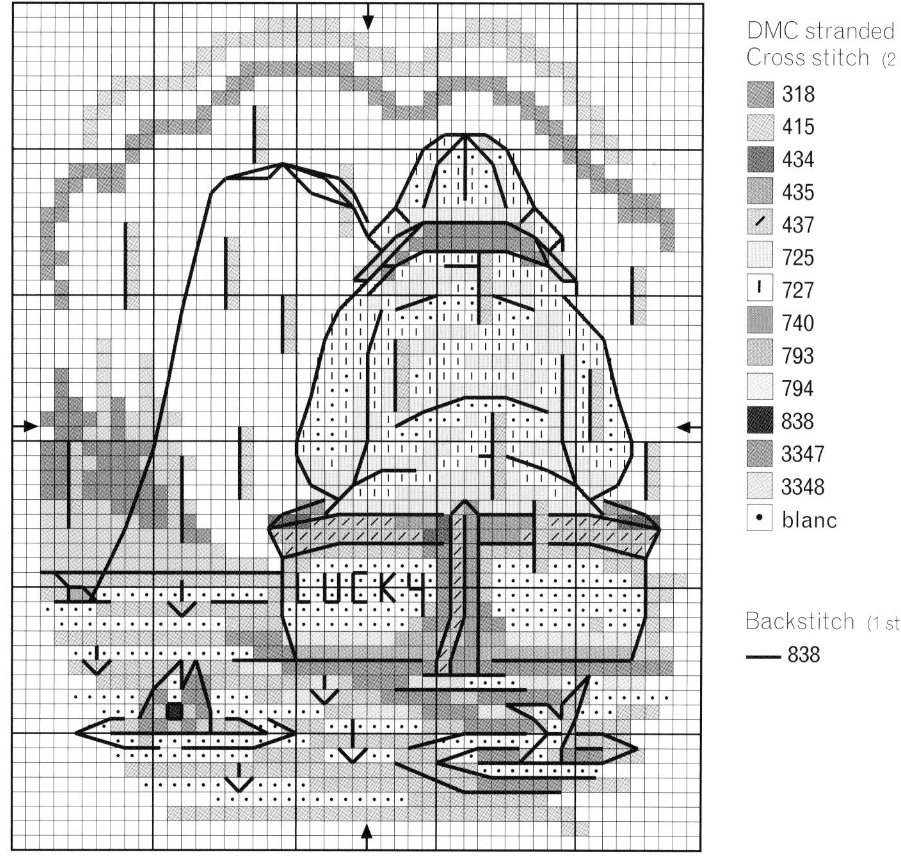

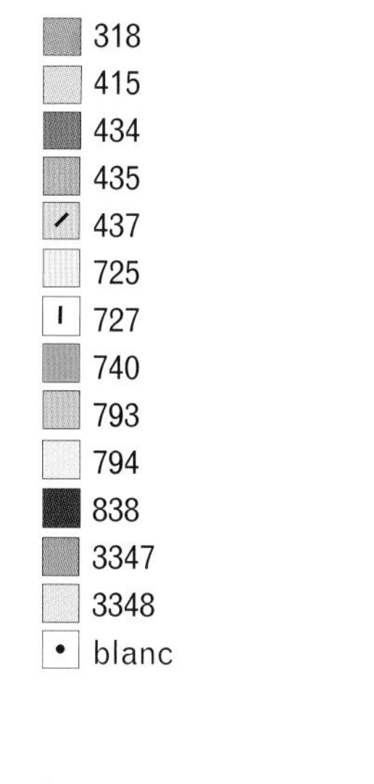

Bags of Love

You will need

14-count cream Aida 20 x 10cm (8 x 4in)

DMC stranded cotton (floss) as listed in chart key plus one skein of 210

Iron-on adhesive

Felt 20 x 36cm (8 x 14in) in lilac and 15cm (6in) square in shocking pink

Cream cotton lace with decorative edge 36cm (14in) long x 1.25cm (½in) wide

String of small pearl-effect beads 71cm (28in)

Two small mother-of-pearl buttons (vintage ones if possible)

Graph paper and tracing/greaseproof paper

Stitch count 68h x 22w (for all 3 motifs)
Design size 12.3 x 4cm (4¾ x 1½in)

This bag is just the right size for a gift of perfume or cosmetics. If you're really short of time, the motifs could be fused to a ready-made bag.

Note Use the measurements above if stitching on a single piece of Aida, or stitch the motifs separately if you have fabric scraps to use up.

To craft the card Iron the adhesive on the back of the stitching (see page 7) and cut out the motifs leaving one square all round each. On a sheet of graph paper draw a rectangle 10.5 x 33cm (4 x 13in), rounding off the top and bottom edges. Draw a rectangle 10.5 x 24.5cm (4⅛ x 9½in), rounding the lower edge. Cut out the patterns, pin to the lilac felt and cut out (no seam allowance needed). Align the lower edges of the front and back, matching curves. Pin together 1.25cm (½in) from the edge, leaving the top open. Using an embroidery needle and six strands of DMC 210, join the front and back with blanket stitch. Neaten the ends of the lace with a few stitches and sew it around the flap edge in toning cotton. Trace the heart template from page 72, pin it on the pink felt, cut out and then pin to the centre front of the flap. Starting at the top middle of the heart sew on the pearl beads. Use the remaining beads for a handle, stitching it to each side. Add two mother-of-pearl buttons at the bottom of the flap. Fuse the other two motifs to the rest of the pink felt. Trim the felt up to the stitching line and attach to the bag with clear glue.

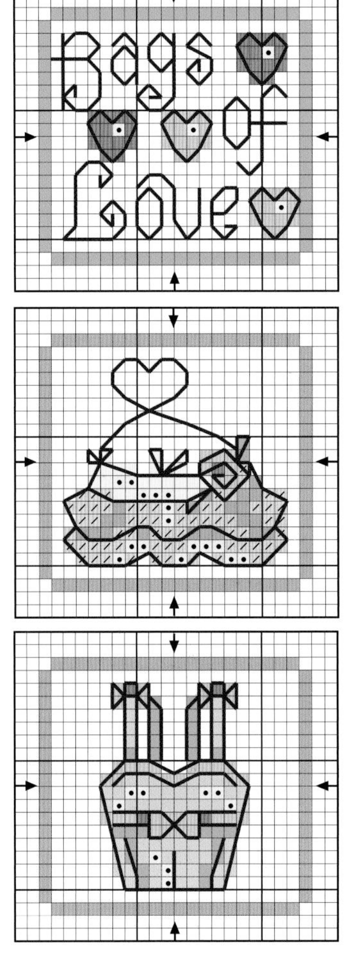

DMC stranded cotton
Cross stitch (2 strands)

- 209
- 211
- 602
- 604
- 727
- 958
- 964
- blanc

Backstitch (1 strand)
838

Shoe Lover

You will need

28-count white evenweave 13cm (5in) square for heart and 13 x 8cm (5 x 3in) for tag

DMC stranded cotton (floss) as listed in chart key

Double-fold card 105 x 148mm (4⅛ x 5¾in) with heart-shaped aperture in white

Clear heart-shaped plastic box to fit aperture (see Suppliers)

Iron-on adhesive

Piece of card for tag 4 x 10.5cm (1½ x 4⅛in) in white

Scallop-edged lace 12cm (4¾in) long x 1.25cm (½in) wide

Ribbon 19cm (7½in) long x 6mm (¼in) wide in pale lilac polka dot

Single hole punch

Stitch count for heart 41h x 46w; for tag 44h x 20w
Design size for heart 7.4 x 8.3cm (3 x 3¼in); for tag 8 x 3.6cm (3⅛ x 1½in)

Note Using the two pieces of evenweave, stitch the motifs separately over two fabric threads.

To craft the card Stick the heart-shaped plastic box into the aperture. Mount the stitching behind the aperture (no wadding). Fix the lace with mini glue dots 2.5cm (1in) above the lower edge, turning the ends to the back. Cut polka dot ribbon the same length as the lace and stick over the top edge of the lace. Iron adhesive on to the back of the tag design and cut out leaving two threads all round. Punch a hole in the white tag card and shape the top edges. Fix the stitching on with double-sided tape. Threading some polka dot ribbon through the hole, knot it, trim ends and stick to the card with mini glue dots.

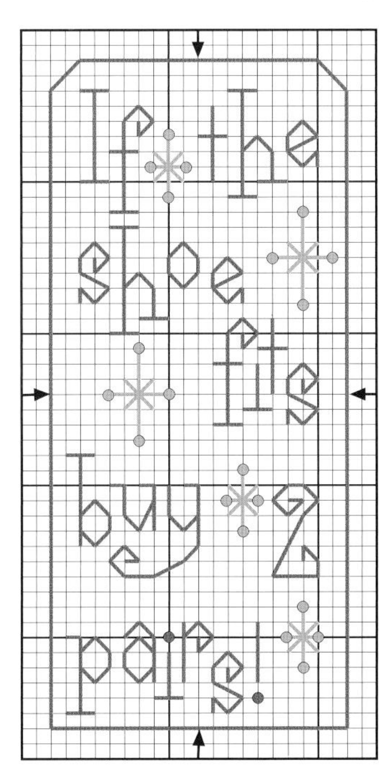

DMC stranded cotton

Cross stitch (2 strands): 151, 415, 210, 3733

Backstitch (1 strand): 3733, 3740

French knots (1 strand): 3733, 3740

Hi Gorgeous!

You will need

28-count white evenweave 20 x 13cm (8 x 5in)

DMC stranded cotton (floss) as listed in chart key

Single-fold card 105 x 210mm (4¼ x 8¼in) in duck-egg blue

Iron-on adhesive

Decorative card 1.5 x 10.5cm (½ x 4¼in) in black polka dot

Die-cut oval 4 x 6cm (1½ x 2¼in) in pale pink

Two pink and pearl flower embellishments

Black sparkle gel pen

Stitch count 83h x 33w
Design size 15 x 6cm (6 x 2⅜in)

Note Remember to stitch over two threads of the evenweave fabric.

To craft the card Iron the adhesive on the back of the stitching (see page 7). Cut out, following the curves and leaving a small amount of evenweave all round (see page 7). Centre the motif 1.25cm (½in) below the top of the card and fix with mini glue dots. Stick the strip of black polka dot card 1.25cm (½in) above the bottom edge using double-sided tape. Write the text or your message on the pink oval or use a suitable peel-off or rub-on greeting to fit. Finish with two pink flower embellishments.

Thirties Vogue

You will need

28-count white evenweave 13 x 10cm (5 x 4in)

DMC stranded cotton (floss) as listed in chart key

Single-fold card 100 x 145mm (4 x 5¾in) in 'Vesuvius' glitter (see Suppliers)

Iron-on adhesive

Piece of white card slightly smaller than finished design

Small foam pads

Stitch count 45h x 35w
Design size 8.2 x 6.4cm (3¼ x 2½in)

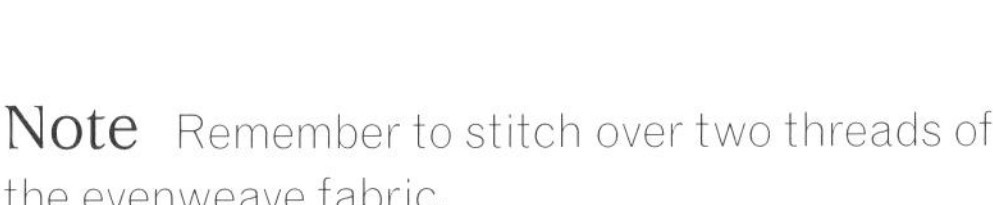

Note Remember to stitch over two threads of the evenweave fabric.

To craft the card Iron the adhesive on to the back of the stitching (see page 7). Cut out around the design leaving two or three threads of evenweave showing. Stick the piece of white card to the back of the design using double-sided tape. Stick small foam pads to this and use these to mount the design on the front of the card. You will find a card on a masculine theme in this Art-Deco style in More Card Ideas on page 77.

Make It Special

Inspired by the covers of 1930s *Vogue* magazine, I deliberately kept the finish of this card simple. Take time to source the perfect card mount to complement your stitching. This gorgeous glitter card has the sophisticated look I wanted and it also echoes all the shades in the design.

Fabulous Forties

You will need

28-count white evenweave 18 x 11cm (7 x 4¼in)

DMC stranded cotton (floss) as listed in chart key

Single-fold card 105 x 210mm (4⅛ x 8¼in) in pale yellow

Iron-on adhesive

Strip of pearlescent card 5 x 21cm (2 x 8¼in) in very pale pink

Strip of decorative card 3.5 x 11cm (1⅜ x 4⅜in) in turquoise and white check

Two die-cut card 'frames' 4cm (1½in) diameter in turquoise

Piece of self-adhesive holographic paper 5 x 10cm (2 x 4in) in silver

Computer generated (or other) text 9.5 x 4.5cm (3¾ x 1¾in)

Small foam pads

Stitch count 67h x 23w
Design size 12 x 4.2cm (4¾ x 1½in)

Make It Special

Stitch the waitress motif and add her to a long, slim gift tag, perhaps in silver, which would be perfect to accompany a gift of champagne!

Note Remember to stitch over two threads of the evenweave fabric.

To craft the card Iron the adhesive on to the back of the stitching (see page 7). Cut out around the design leaving two threads of fabric all round. Using double-sided tape, fix the pink pearlescent card strip down the right side of the card and the checked card strip across the bottom. Position the text box just below the top. Cut two circles from holographic paper slightly smaller than the die-cut frames. Stick them on the pink card below the text. Mount the two frames on top using mini glue dots. Use foam pads to stick the waitress to the card.

DMC stranded cotton
Cross stitch (2 strands)

- 415
- 597
- 598
- 747
- 754
- 758
- 838
- 919
- 922
- 948
- blanc

Backstitch (1 strand)

- 838
- 3801

French knots (1 strand)

- 838

I used computer-generated text (Brush Script 16pt) in turquoise to make my greeting (see page 9). If you prefer, make a box by cutting a piece of white card the same size. Use stick-on alphabet letters in really bright colours to give the look of a vintage fluorescent sign. The die-cut frames for the porthole windows came from a single really useful pack of assorted shapes, which you will see I've used throughout the book!

Rock 'n' Roll Fifties

You will need

14-count cream Aida 15 x 20cm (6 x 8in)

DMC stranded cotton (floss) as listed in chart key

Single-fold card 150 x 210mm (6 x 8¼in) in palest aqua pearlescent embossed check

Iron-on adhesive

Assorted die-cut shapes – two ovals 4 x 6cm (1½ x 2⅜in) in bright pink and pale yellow; an oval 'frame' 5 x 8cm (2 x 3in) in turquoise; three circles 3cm (1⅛in) diameter in bright pink, pale green and pale yellow (optional)

Stitch count 55h x 74w
Design size 10 x 13.5cm (4 x 5¼in)

Note Use the measurements above if stitching the motifs on a single piece of Aida or stitch the motifs separately if you have fabric scraps to use up.

To craft the card

Iron the adhesive on to the back of the stitching (see page 7). Cut out the motifs following the designs leaving one or two blocks all round (see page 7). Cut out the stars as small squares. Using double-sided tape, stick the lettering above the lower edge of the card. Arrange your motifs on the card with the die-cut shapes – refer to the picture or do your own design. Attach all the various elements using mini glue dots.

DMC stranded cotton

Cross stitch (2 strands)

318
350
415
434
435
437
725
727
741
838
956
957
959
964
blanc

Backstitch (1 strand)

838
959

World's Greatest Cross-Stitcher

You will need

14-count cream Aida 15cm (6in) square

DMC stranded cotton (floss) as listed in chart key

Single-fold card 148mm (5¾in) square in lilac

Iron-on adhesive

Small cross stitch chart about 9cm (3½in) square (see Make it Special, below)

Six 8cm (3½in) lengths of DMC 209, 211, 727, 956, 957 and 3340

Self-adhesive ribbon 17cm (6½in) long x 6mm (¼in) wide in pale pink

Single hole punch

Small foam pads

Stitch count 55h x 53w
Design size 10 x 9.6cm (4 x 3¾in)

To craft the card Iron the adhesive on the back of the stitching (see page 7). Cut out the motif leaving two squares all round. Punch a hole 2cm (¾in) from the top of the card. Repeat five times, spacing evenly so the edge resembles a thread card. Use mini glue dots to fix the cross stitch chart in place (you could photocopy the one on page 72). Stick the stitching in place with foam pads. Fix the ribbon down the side of the card. Tie the threads through the holes to finish.

Make It Special

I used a reduced computer printout of my original design as a special touch. Photocopy the one on page 72 or use a chart from a magazine or make your own by drawing symbols on graph paper. If you prefer, add some little stitching charms instead. This card would be great to accompany a present of stitching materials or to hold a gift voucher for a favourite craft shop.

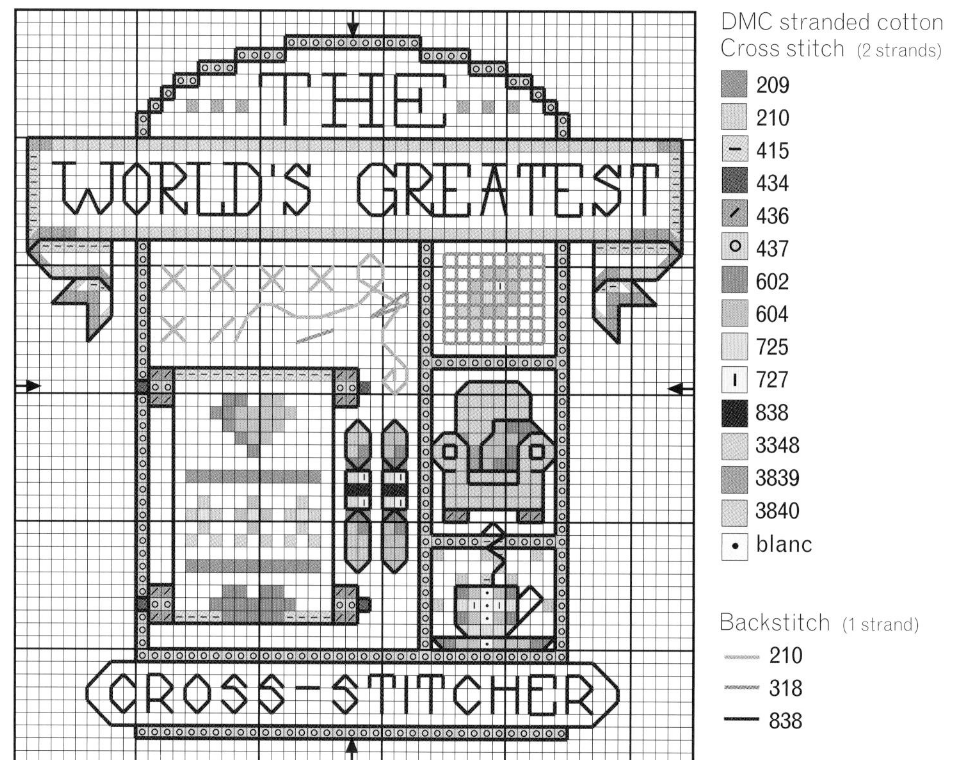

World's Greatest Gardener

You will need

14-count cream Aida 15cm (6in) square

DMC stranded cotton (floss) as listed in chart key

Single-fold card 148mm (5¾in) square in mid blue

Iron-on adhesive

Self-adhesive ribbon 17cm (6½in) long x 6mm (¼in) wide in yellow gingham

Small piece of sunflower yellow card and scrap of bright orange for punching

Small flower punch and a single hole punch

Stitch count 55h x 53w
Design size 10 x 9.6cm (4 x 3¾in)

To craft the card Iron the adhesive on the back of the stitching (see page 7). Cut out the motif leaving two squares all round. Stick the self-adhesive ribbon down the right side of the card 4cm (1½in) from the edge. Punch three flowers from yellow card and three centres from orange card. Stick the centres to the flowers with mini glue dots and stipple them with a fine black pen. Fix the first flower in place 1.25cm (½in) from the top edge with a mini glue dot. Fix the other two flowers, spacing equally. Fix the stitching on using mini glue dots.

You'll find more 'World's Greatest' motifs on pages 72–73. To save space I've shown the banner separately to the rest of the motifs. Align the stitches at the top of the frame on the main part of the design with the two stitches shown just below the banner to match them up. Use the chart on this page to check the exact position.

DMC stranded cotton
Cross stitch (2 strands)

- 322
- 352
- 415
- 434
- 435
- 437
- 721
- 725
- 727
- 739
- 817
- 3325
- 3345
- 3347
- 3348
- blanc

Backstitch (1 strand)

- 838
- 3345

HAPPY BIRTHDAY!

DMC stranded cotton
Cross stitch (2 strands)

415	604	959	3805
445	798	964	3853
553	838	3746	blanc

Backstitch (1 strand)

838

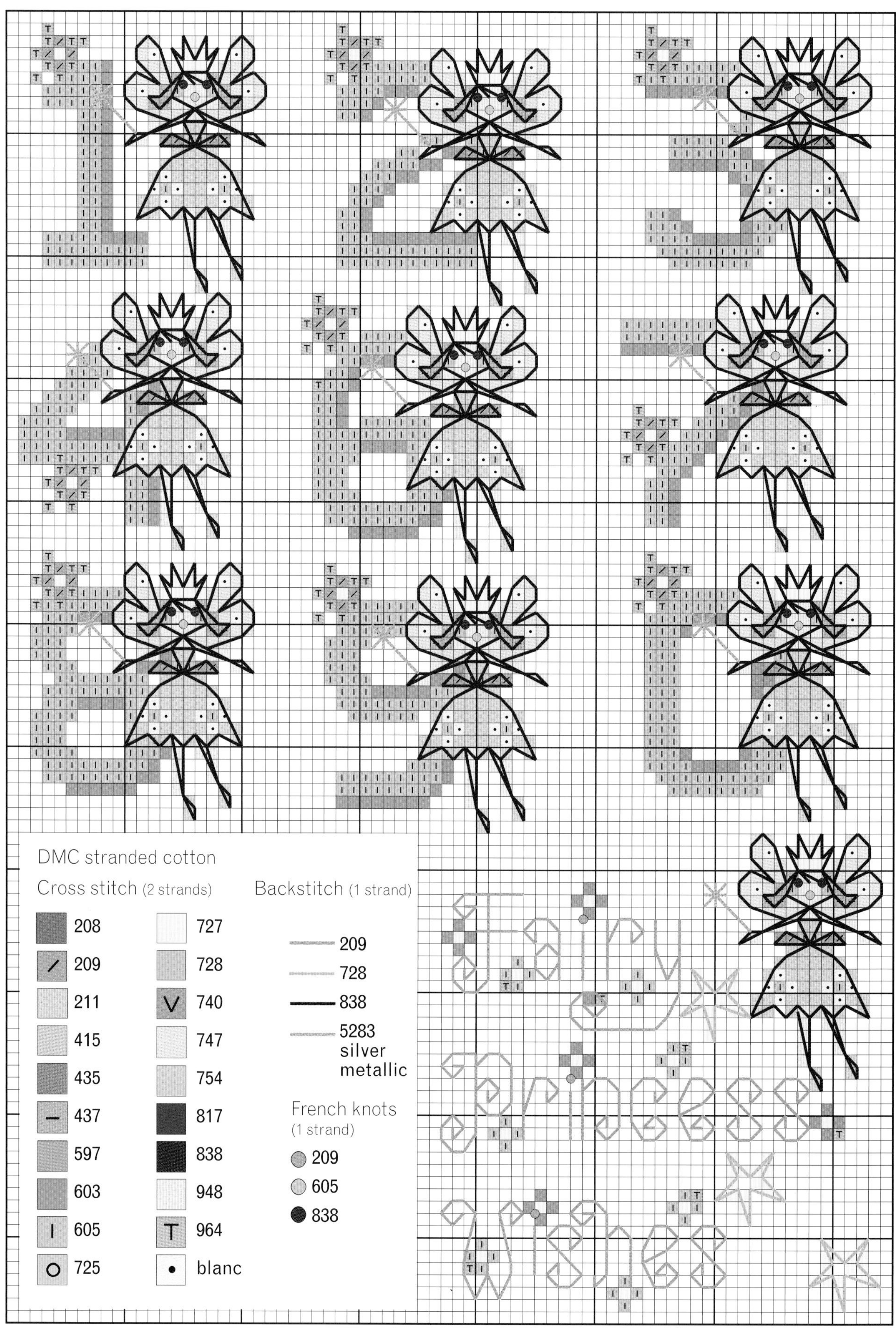
DMC stranded cotton
Cross stitch (2 strands)
208
/ 209
211
415
435
– 437
597
603
I 605
O 725
727
728
V 740
747
754
817
838
948
T 964
• blanc
Backstitch (1 strand)
209
728
838
5283 silver metallic
French knots (1 strand)
209
605
838

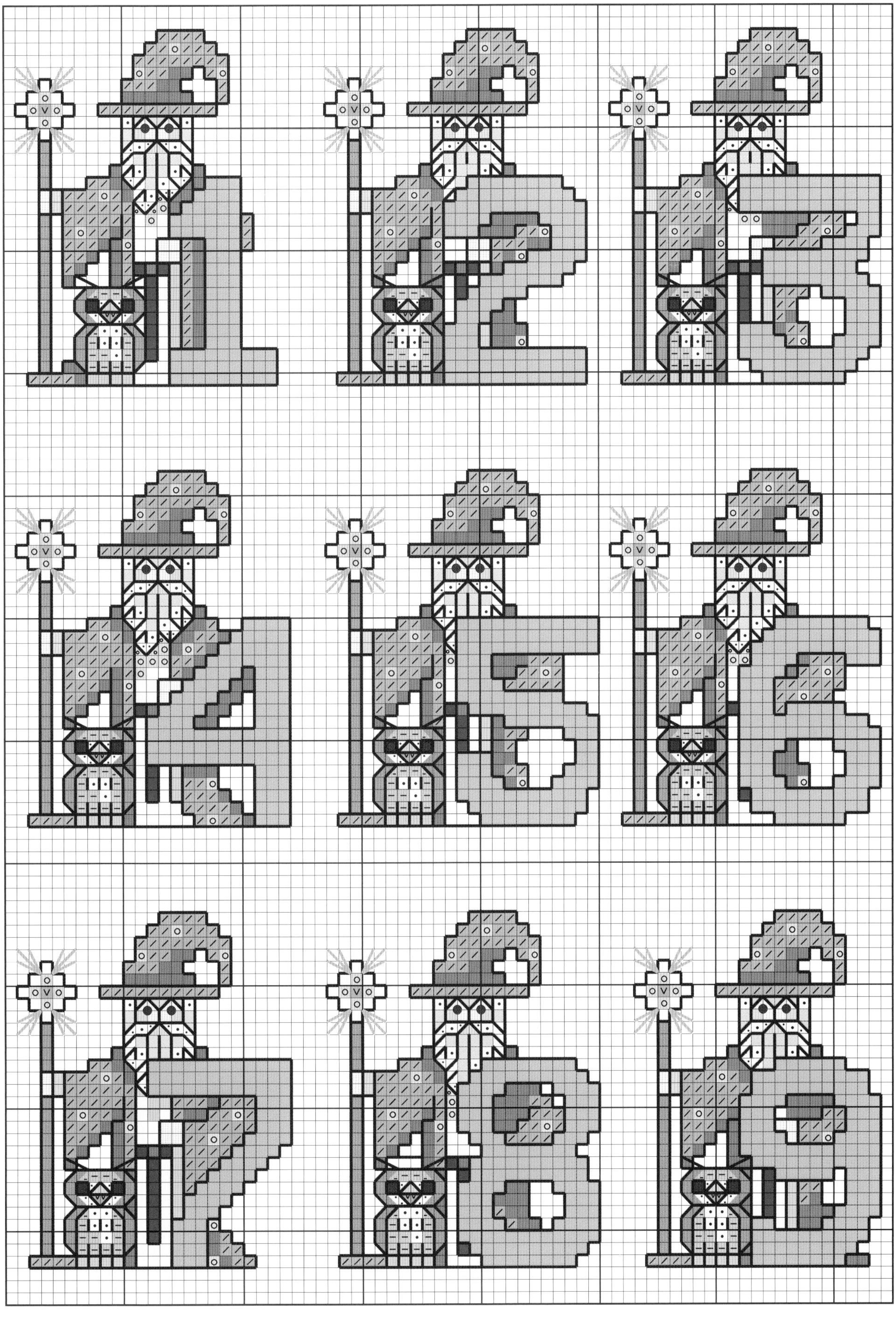

World's Greatest Cross-Stitcher

Symbol chart for photocopying

Bags of Love

Heart Template
actual size

Love me Love my CAT!!

CAT-LOVER

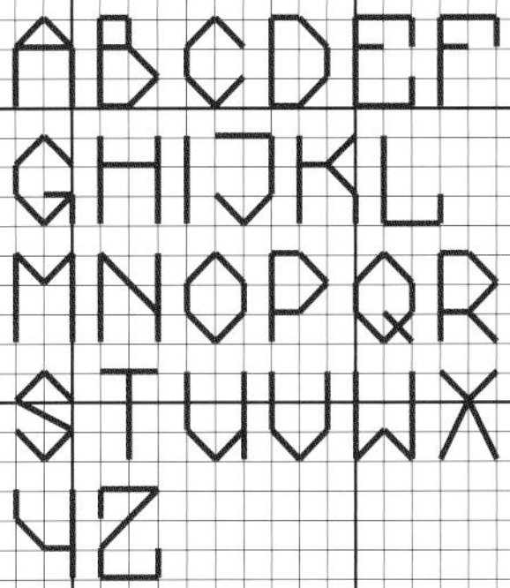

ABCDEF
GHIJKL
MNOPQR
STUVWX
YZ

CHOCOHOLIC

DMC stranded cotton

Cross stitch (2 strands)

Symbol	DMC	Symbol	DMC
	208	+	613
/	210		725
	317	O	727
I	318		838
	322		948
	350		956
\	352	L	957
	415		3347
•	433		3348
	434	–	3755
	435		3761
	437		3771
T	612	•	blanc

Backstitch (1 strand)

—— 838

French knots (1 strand)

● 838

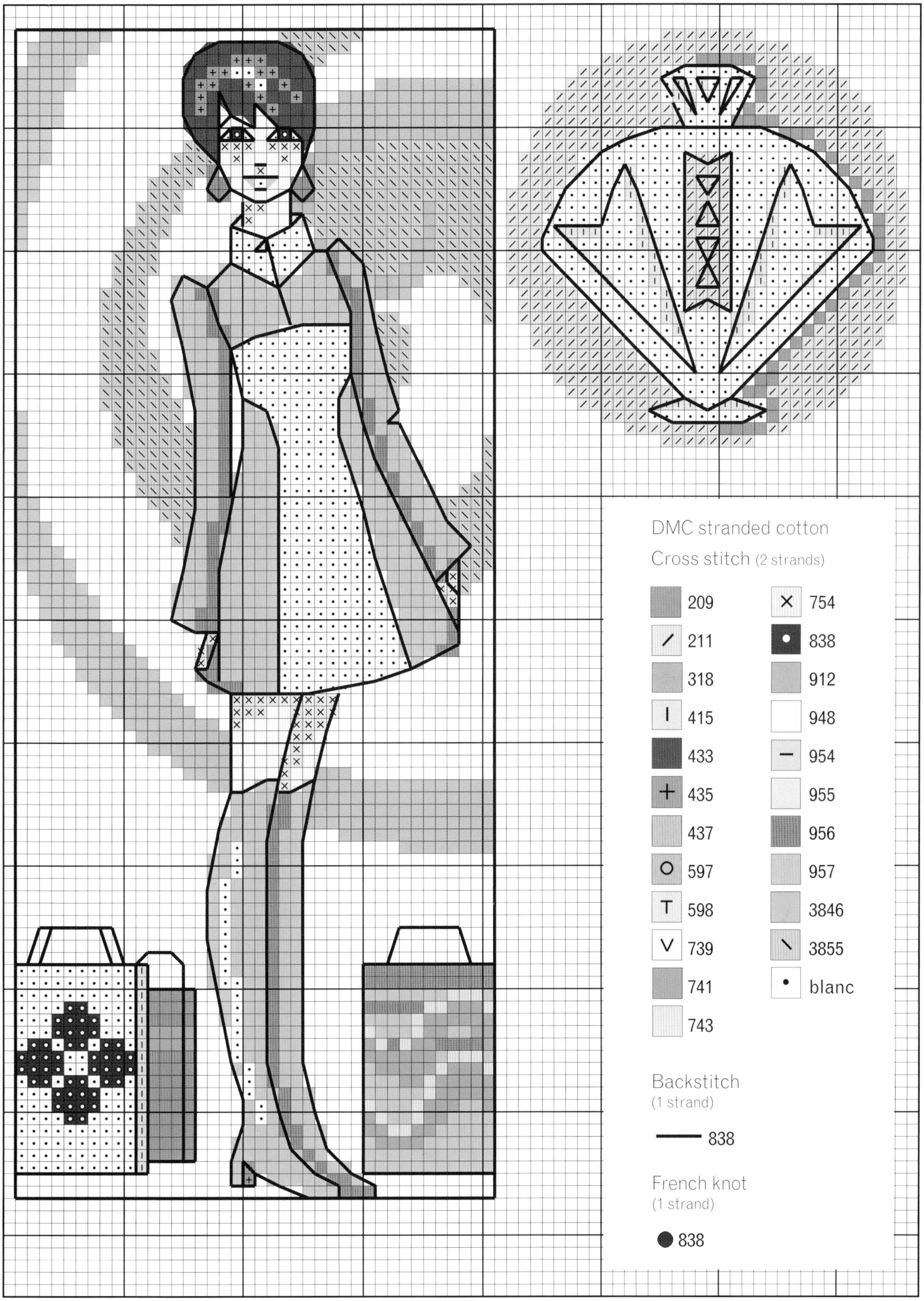

DMC stranded cotton

Cross stitch (2 strands)

Symbol	DMC	Symbol	DMC
	209	×	754
/	211	•	838
	318		912
I	415		948
	433	–	954
+	435		955
	437		956
O	597		957
T	598		3846
V	739	\	3855
	741	•	blanc
	743		

Backstitch
(1 strand)

— 838

French knot
(1 strand)

● 838

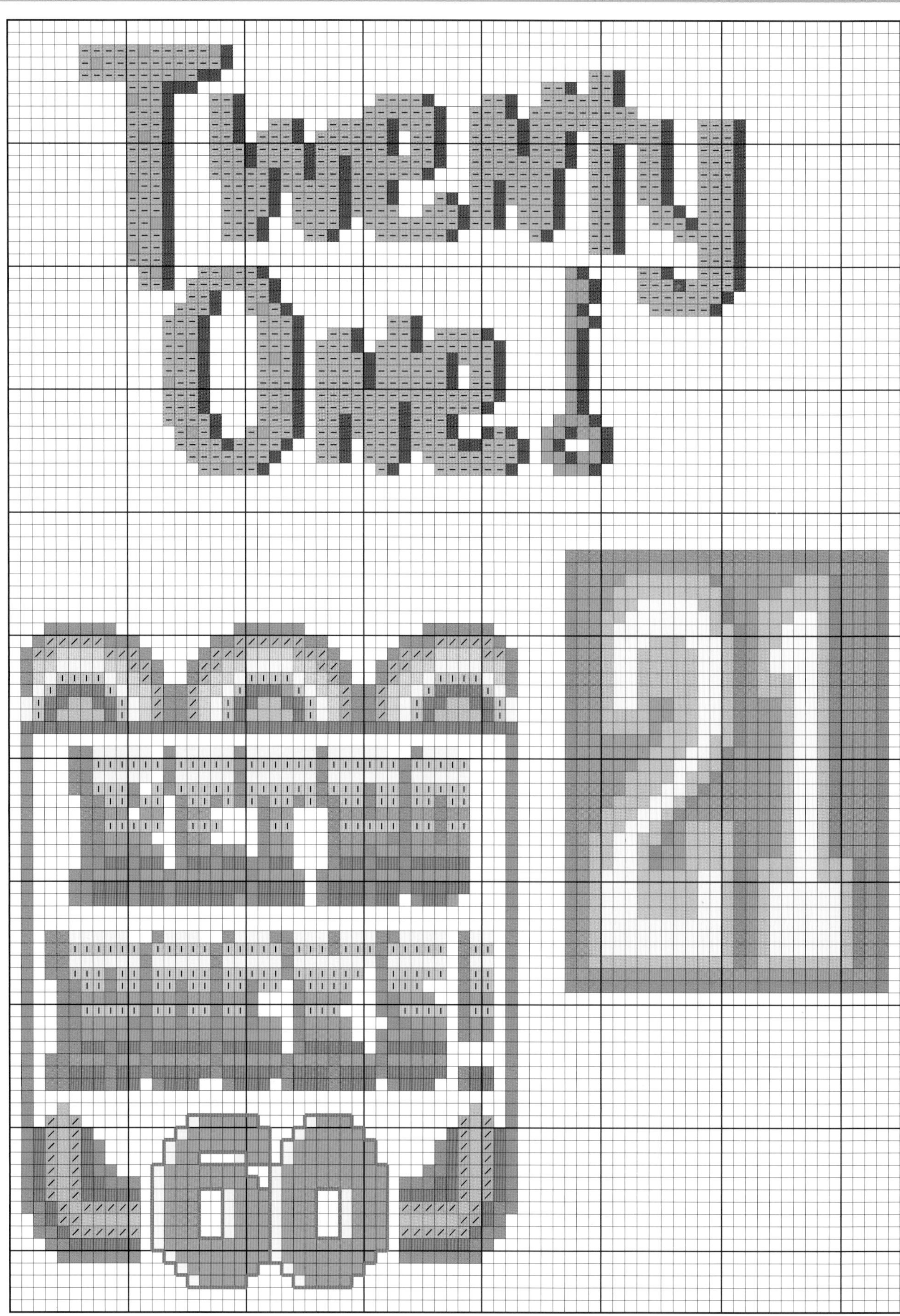

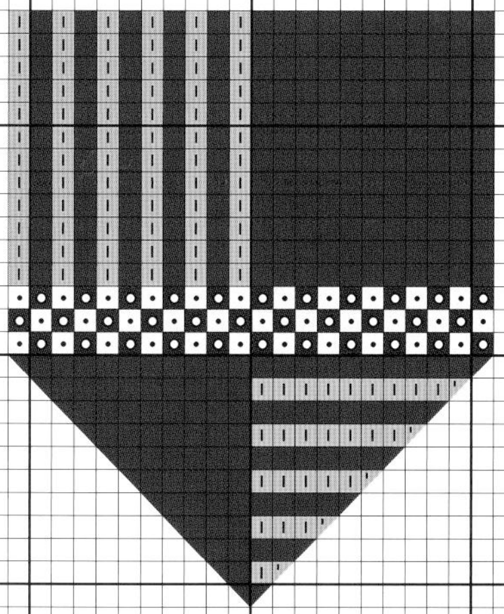

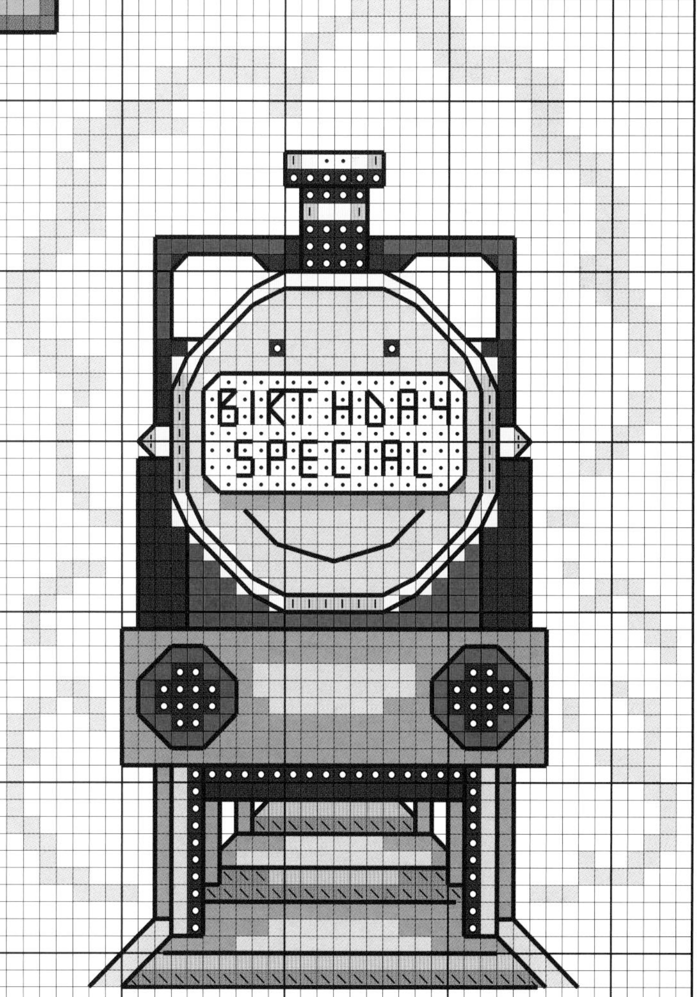

DMC stranded cotton

Cross stitch (2 strands)

Symbol	DMC	Symbol	DMC
	208		726
/	209		740
	211	×	747
	318		816
	350	•	838
	415		955
	434		3041
\	435	○	3042
	437	–	3811
	597	I	3820
	602	•	blanc

Backstitch (1 strand)

- 208
- 838

Seasonal Favourites

Mark the passing seasons by making some fabulous quick-to-stitch cards to celebrate high days and holidays. Start the year by making a gorgeous valentine card or keepsake for someone special to treasure. Add to the enjoyment of Easter with some lovely flowery designs bright with the promise of spring. Or make the gift of a chocolate egg even more delicious with a pretty tag.

Show appreciation for your parents on Mother's or Father's Day with the gift of a keepsake book ready to fill with special memories. If you prefer to give cards, a gorgeous posy adorns a handbag-shaped card for Mum, while a humorous motif invites Dad to chill out. You'll also find designs to celebrate some of the best-known patron saint days as well as the 4th of July holiday, all designed to cheer anyone proud of their homeland. Why not include a Hallowe'en card featuring a not-so-scary ghost or a quick-to-stitch pumpkin motif in your autumn stitching? Finally, get ready for Christmas with a trio of festive cards and an easy to make angel ornament.

Check out the extra motifs on pages 96–103 for even more inspiration, such as the fun Christmas designs and a multitude of gift tag designs, guaranteed to keep you busy stitching throughout the year.

DAD
RELAX
chill
snooze

Fathers
Are
Special

Hearts and Swans

You will need

28-count white evenweave 18cm (7in) square

DMC stranded cotton (floss) as listed in chart key

Single-fold card 145mm (5¾in) square in 'vino' (burgundy) cord texture (see Suppliers)

Iron-on adhesive

Pre-gathered lace 33cm (13in) long x 6mm (¼in) wide in white

Four self-adhesive diamantes 3mm (⅛in) in pale pink

Small ready-made ribbon bow 2.5cm (1in) in white

Clear glue and mini glue dots

Stitch count 52h x 65w
Design size 9.5 x 11.5 x 9.6cm (3¾ x 4½in)

Note Remember to stitch over two threads of the evenweave fabric.

To craft the card

Iron the adhesive on to the back of the stitching (see page 7). Leave the backing in place and draw a heart shape about 6mm (¼in) from the stitching around just one side of the design. Cut it out beginning at the top. Remove the backing paper, fold the motif in half and use the shape as a template to cut out the other side. Beginning at centre top, stick the lace around the heart using clear glue (leave until slightly tacky before starting), folding the end under neatly. When dry, stick the heart to the card. Add a bow with mini glue dots and finish with a diamante in each corner.

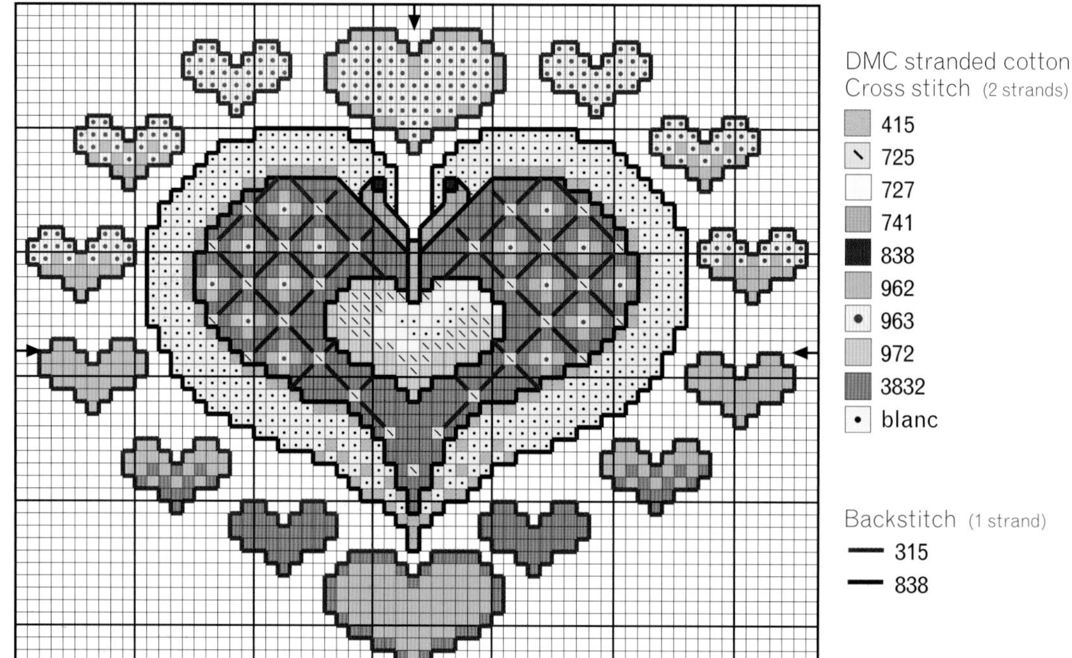

Glasgow Rose Trinket Box

You will need

28-count white evenweave 15cm (6in) square

DMC stranded cotton (floss) as listed in chart key

Wooden box with clasp 10 x 15cm (4 x 6in) (see Suppliers)

Iron-on adhesive

Folk Art acrylic paint in light fuchsia

Paintbrush

Clear glue

Stitch count 43h x 56w
Design size 7.8 x 10.2cm (3 x 4in)

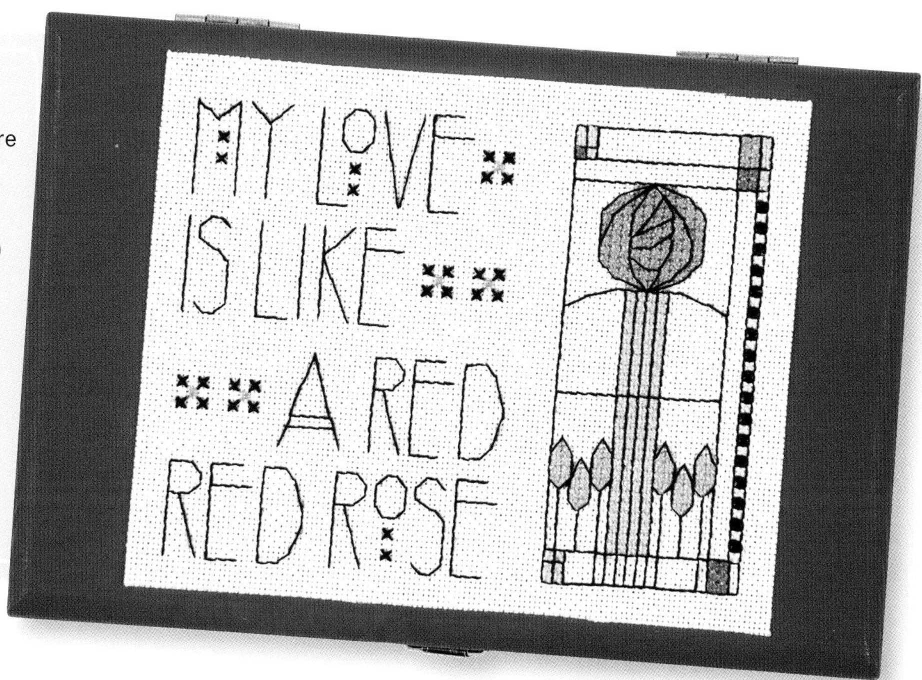

Note Remember to stitch over two threads of the evenweave fabric.

To craft the card Iron the adhesive on to the back of the stitching (see page 7). With the paper backing in place, measure 6mm (¼in) from the widest points of the design. Use a ruler and pencil to mark the border and cut along this line to create a straight edge to the motif. Paint the box (you may need to sand it down between coats) and allow to dry before fixing the stitching in place with a thin layer of clear glue.

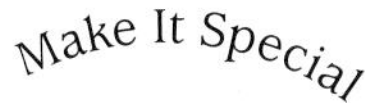
Make It Special

This design would look even more stylish if it was edged in narrow black or dark burgundy velvet ribbon. The rose motif could be used separately for a card.

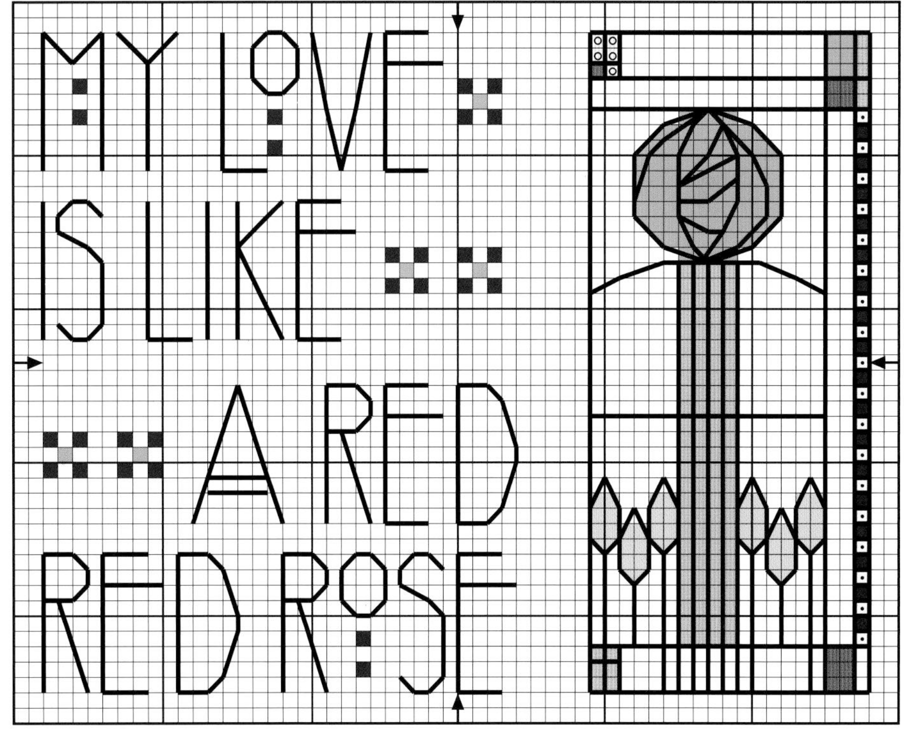

DMC stranded cotton

Cross stitch (2 strands)		Backstitch (1 strand)
164	3689	— 310
310	3743	
3687	blanc	
3688		

Spring Tulip

You will need

14-count white Aida 10 x 18cm (4 x 7in)

DMC stranded cotton (floss) as listed in chart key

Single-fold card 70 x 185mm ($2\frac{3}{4}$ x $7\frac{1}{4}$in) in pale green

Iron-on adhesive

Double-sided tape

Self-adhesive daisy embellishments, two each of lilac, pink and yellow and three of white (optional)

Stitch count 70h x 16w
Design size 12.7 x 3cm (5 x $1\frac{1}{8}$in)

To craft the card Iron the adhesive on to the back of the stitching (see page 7). Cut out the design leaving four squares of Aida all round. Carefully fray the edges (use tweezers) until you have a border of two squares of Aida around the design. Use double-sided tape to attach the motif to the card and finish off with a scattering of daisy embellishments.

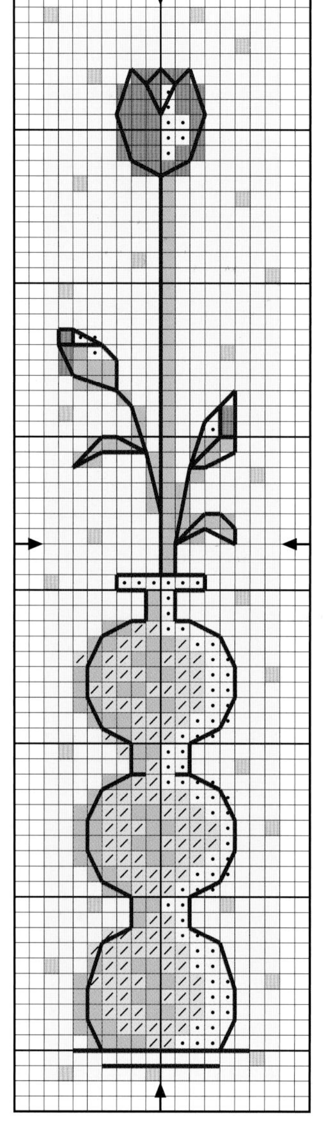

The lovely fresh colours and contemporary look of this card also make it perfect for a spring birthday or Mother's Day. Used as a get well card it's sure to cheer up the recipient. Choose a brighter coloured card and add a zingy mulberry paper layer to give a more quirky style.

XXX

The linear style of the motif would also work well stitched up as a bookmark with a felt backing.

XXX

The tulip motif would suit the cover of a gardening notebook – perhaps one containing your notes on which spring bulbs to order.

DMC stranded cotton
Cross stitch (2 strands)

- 211
- 445
- 907
- 956
- 959
- / 964
- • blanc

Backstitch (1 strand)

— 838

Floral Egg

You will need

28-count white evenweave 15cm (6in) square

DMC stranded cotton (floss) as listed in chart key

Single-fold card 105 x 147mm (4⅛ x 5¾in) in soft pink

Iron-on adhesive

Strip of card 3.8 x 25.5cm (1½ x 10in) in pale lemon

Self-adhesive satin ribbon 30.5cm (12in) long x 6mm (¼in) wide in pale green

Organza ribbon 30.5cm (12in) long x 2cm (¾in) wide in palest pink

Scrap of self-adhesive satin ribbon 6mm (¼in) wide in pale pink (for centre of bow)

Mini glue dots

Double-sided tape

Stitch count 53h x 43w
Design size 9.6 x 7.8cm (3¾ x 3in)

Note Remember to stitch over two threads of the evenweave fabric.

To craft the card Iron the adhesive on the back of the stitching (see page 7). Cut out the motif in an egg shape, leaving about 6mm (¼in) of fabric all around. Cut the pale lemon card the same width as the single-fold card and the remaining strip to the same length as the card. Trim the edges of the strips with the self-adhesive green ribbon. Fix these strips to the card with double-sided tape. Use glue dots to fix the stitching on top. Cut the organza ribbon in half and loop one piece into a bow. Take a stitch through the centre, pull tight and wind the cotton round several times to form a bow shape. Repeat with the other piece of ribbon. Take a stitch through the centre of each to make a double bow. Trim the ends of the bows and finish the centre by wrapping with pink ribbon. Attach the bow using mini glue dots. Follow the chart on page 96 to stitch a matching gift tag.

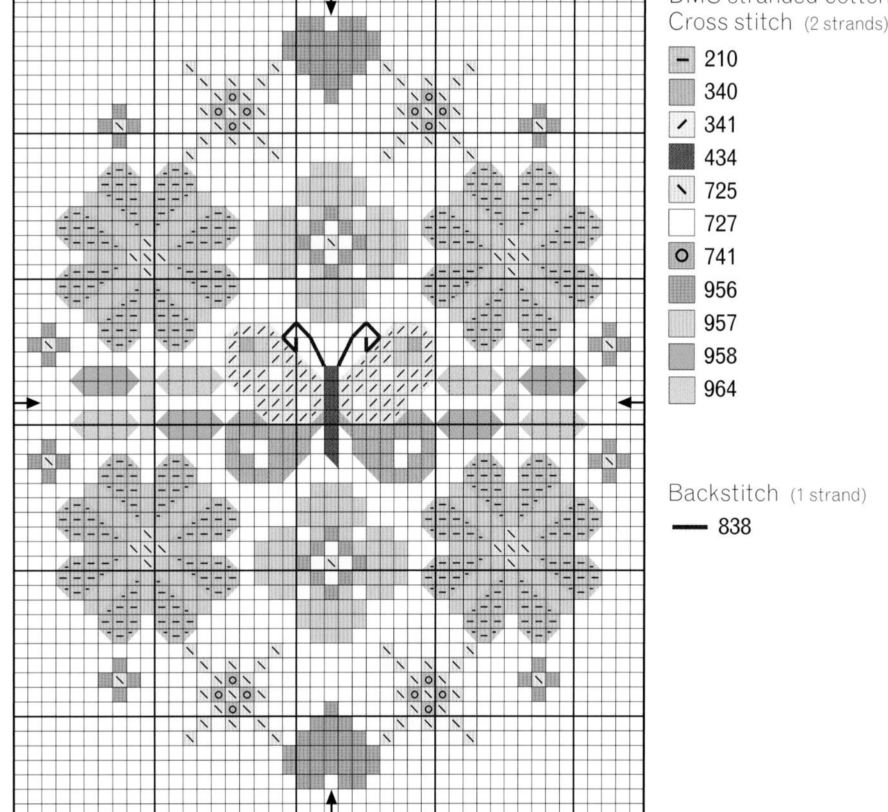

St Patrick's Day

You will need

14-count cream Aida 15cm (6in) square

DMC stranded cotton (floss) as listed in chart key

Single-fold card 105 x 147mm (4⅛ x 5¾in) in pale gold

Iron-on adhesive

Piece of card 2.5 x 9cm (1 x 3½in) in deep green

Self-adhesive ribbon 10.5cm (4⅛in) long x 6mm (¼in) wide in green gingham

Mini glue dots

Gold pen

Stitch count 61h x 50w
Design size 11 x 9cm (4½ x 3½in)

To craft the card Iron the adhesive on to the back of the stitching (see page 7). Cut out leaving one square of Aida round the design and a smooth curve around the rainbow. With mini glue dots, fix the motif on the card so the curve extends slightly above it. Stick the ribbon about 2.5cm (1in) above the lower edge of the card. I used a gold metallic pen to write the lettering on the green card but you could use gold stick-on letters. Fix the green card on top of the ribbon with mini glue dots. Your card is now ready for St Patrick's Day on 17 March.

If you don't have time to stitch the whole card, just use the cute angel motif (without the gold ribbon). Stick her to a small gold or toning green card and maybe add a rainbow button or shamrock charm.

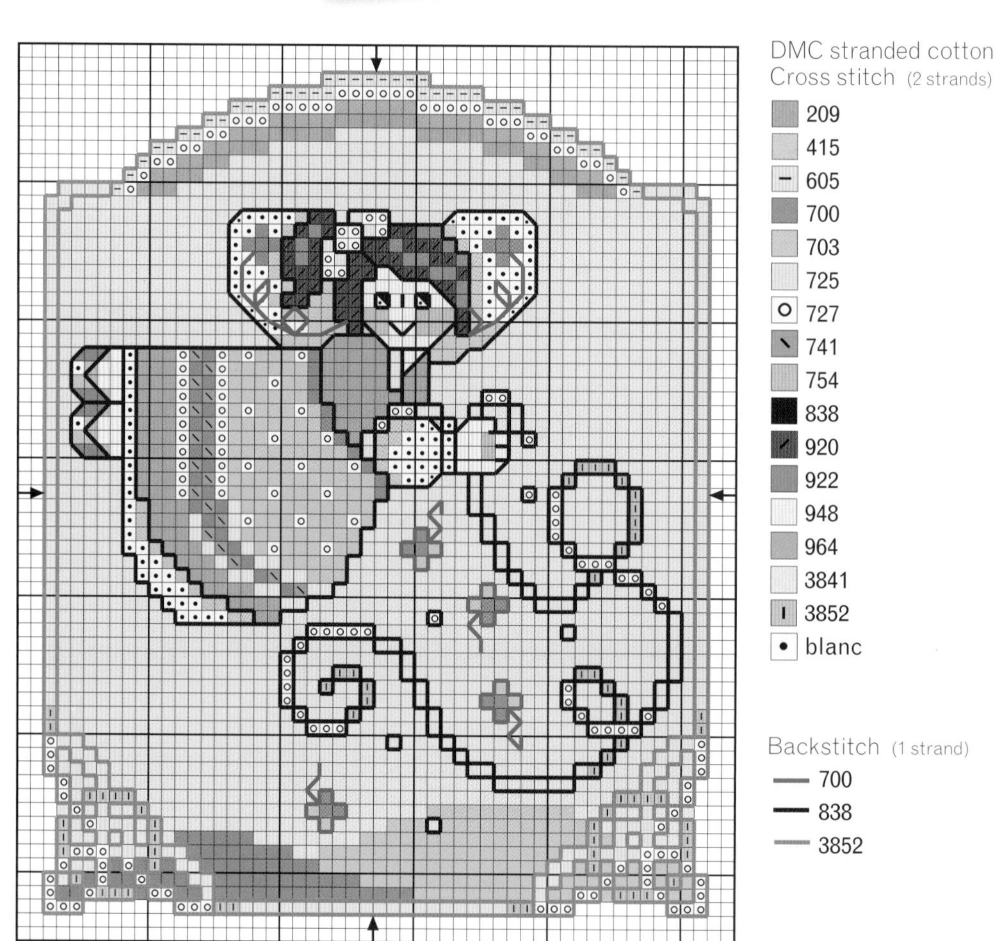

DMC stranded cotton
Cross stitch (2 strands)

- 209
- 415
- 605
- 700
- 703
- 725
- 727
- 741
- 754
- 838
- 920
- 922
- 948
- 964
- 3841
- 3852
- blanc

Backstitch (1 strand)

- 700
- 838
- 3852

St Andrew's Day

You will need

14-count cream Aida 15cm (6in) square

DMC stranded cotton (floss) as listed in chart key

Single-fold card 117mm (4½in) square in lilac

Iron-on adhesive

Mini glue dots

Stitch count 54h x 54w
Design size 9.8cm (3¾in) square

To craft the card Iron the adhesive on to the back of the stitching (see page 7). Cut out the design leaving one square of Aida all round and giving a smooth look to the corners by cutting them diagonally. Draw a diagonal line across the right-hand corners of the card and trim them to echo the motif shape. Use glue dots to attach the design to the card – perfect for St Andrew's Day on 30 November.

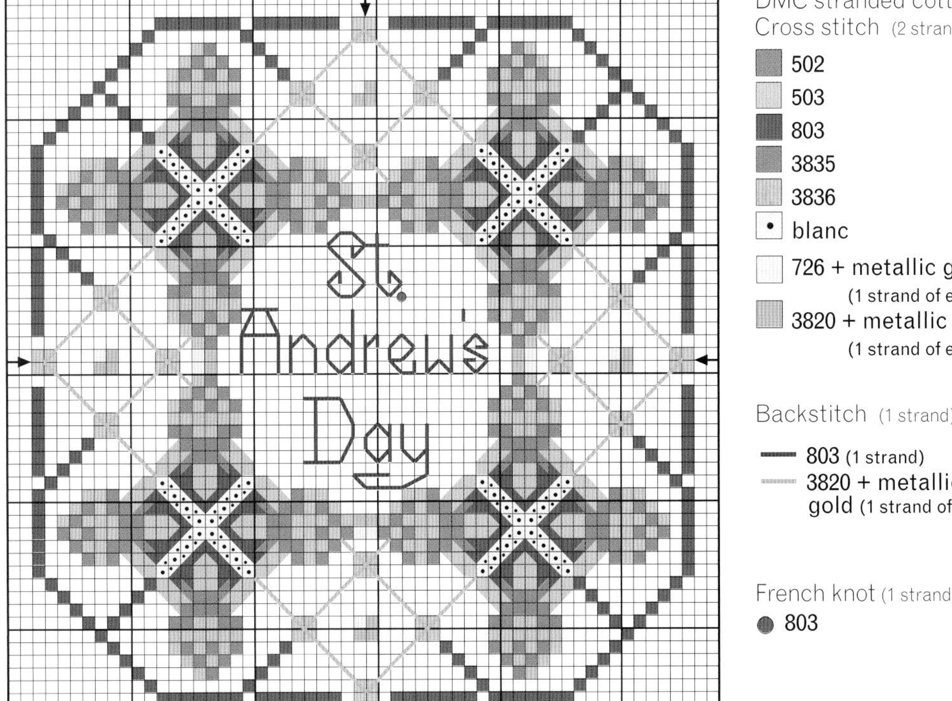

DMC stranded cotton
Cross stitch (2 strands)

- 502
- 503
- 803
- 3835
- 3836
- blanc
- 726 + metallic gold (1 strand of each)
- 3820 + metallic gold (1 strand of each)

Backstitch (1 strand)

- 803 (1 strand)
- 3820 + metallic gold (1 strand of each)

French knot (1 strand)

- 803

St David's Day

I chose the patron saint of my homeland, St David, to make this little card. The yellow of the daffodil stands out brightly against misty Welsh mountains and is echoed in the colour of the card. To finish off I added the Welsh legend 'Cymru am Byth' which means 'Wales Forever'. St David's Day is celebrated on 1 March. The chart for this appears in More Card Ideas on page 96 – why not stitch the red cross design on page 96 for St George's Day on 23 April?

Mum's Keepsake Book

You will need

28-count white evenweave 15cm (6in) square

DMC stranded cotton (floss) as listed in chart key

K & Co mini-book 13 x 18cm (5⅛ x 7in) (see Suppliers)

Iron-on adhesive

Piece of card 10.5cm (4⅛in) square in pale blue

Mini glue dots

Stitch count 51h x 53w
Design size 9.3 x 9.6cm (3½ x 3¾in)

Note Remember to stitch over two threads of the evenweave fabric.

To craft the card Iron the adhesive on to the back of the stitching (see page 7). Cut out the motif leaving two or three threads of evenweave all round. Use mini glue dots to stick it to the blue card. Attach the design to the book cover using mini glue dots.

Make It Special

The book cover inspired the style and colours of this motif but it would look equally good on a plainer surface. Look out for ordinary notebooks that can be prettied up by covering with decorative paper and adding embellishments such as ribbon ties or buttons. To make it extra special why not fill a few pages of the book with keepsakes such as family snapshots and special verses or sayings?

DMC stranded cotton
Cross stitch (2 strands)

- 437
- 712
- 739
- 813
- 818
- 826
- 838
- 956
- 957
- 3348
- blanc
- 725 + Kreinik 091 (1 strand of each)
- 727 + Kreinik 091 (1 strand of each)
- 972 + Kreinik 091 (1 strand of each)

Backstitch (1 strand)

- 825
- 838
- 3346
- 3820

Posy Handbag

You will need

14-count cream 13cm (5in) square

DMC stranded cotton (floss) as listed in chart key

Die-cut handbag card in pearlescent pale lilac (see Suppliers)

Iron-on adhesive

Rectangle of card 4.5 x 6.5cm (1¾ x 2½in) in pearlescent ivory

Circle of card 4cm (1½in) diameter

Small piece of pale green felt

Pre-gathered lace 11cm (4½in) long x 6mm (¼in) wide in white

Grosgrain ribbon 20cm (8in) long x 6mm (¼in) wide in pale lilac

Two small self-adhesive flower gems in pale pink (optional)

Strip of self-adhesive daisies 14cm (5½in) long x 6mm (¼in) wide in pale lilac

Stitch count 30h x 55w
Design size 5.5 x 10cm (2⅛ x 4in)

Use beads on some of the flower petals for a special look. If you don't want to use the handbag shape then stitch more flowers and use the same method to make a larger posy to use as a card topper.

For a quick and pretty project, stitch a different coloured flower for each window of a triple-aperture card.

Note Use the measurements above if stitching on a single piece of fabric. I used scraps of Aida in pale blue, pink and lemon for a vintage look.

To craft the card Iron the adhesive on the back of the stitching (see page 7). Cut out the flower shapes. Cut out the tag and fix it with glue dots to the rectangle of card. Trim the top corners of the card and punch a hole in the centre. Thread 8.5cm (3¼in) of grosgrain ribbon through and tie. Use clear glue to stick the lace to the back of the card circle, overlapping ends neatly. Fold the remaining ribbon in half and glue in place. Cut three leaf shapes from felt and stick them on the card circle with glue dots. Fix the flowers in place and add the flower gems. Stick a strip of daisies across the bag front and single daisies on the handle. Finally, fix the tag with a glue dot.

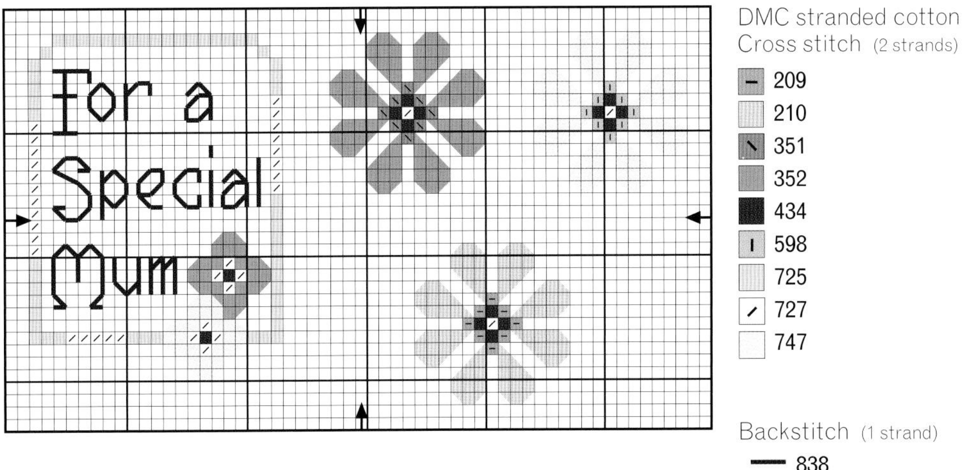

DMC stranded cotton
Cross stitch (2 strands)

- 209
- 210
- 351
- 352
- 434
- 598
- 725
- 727
- 747

Backstitch (1 strand)

- 838

Dad's Keepsake Book

You will need

28-count white evenweave 13cm (5in) square

DMC stranded cotton (floss) as listed in chart key

Circular mini-book 11cm (4¼in) diameter with plain board covers and screw fixing (see Suppliers)

Iron-on adhesive

Piece of green plaid decorative paper 13cm (5in) square

Six small leaves and two acorn embellishments (optional)

Mini glue dots and clear glue

Single hole punch

Stitch count 42w x 42h
Design size 7.6cm (3in) square

Note Remember to stitch over two threads of the evenweave fabric.

To craft the card Iron the adhesive on to the back of the stitching (see page 7). Cut out the motif close to the edge of the stitching leaving a small amount of fabric all round. Use the book cover as a template to cut out the same shape in plaid paper. Mark the hole for the book's screw fixing with a pencil and then punch a single hole. Stick the paper smoothly on to the board cover using clear glue. Position the motif on top and attach using mini glue dots. Finish by adding leaf and acorn embellishments using glue dots.

DMC stranded cotton
Cross stitch (2 strands)

- 435
- 437
- 3347
- 3348
- 3766
- Madeira gold No 20 shade 9812 (1 strand)

Backstitch (1 strand)

- 838

Chilled-Out Dad

You will need

14-count cream Aida 15cm (6in) square

DMC stranded cotton (floss) as listed in chart key

Single-fold card 105 x 210mm (4 x 8¼in) in 'Elf' (pale green) cord texture (see Suppliers)

Iron-on adhesive

Piece of card 10.5cm (4in) square in orange cord texture

Self-adhesive 'jelly' alphabet stickers

Mini glue dots

Stitch count 53h x 50w
Design size 10 x 9cm (4 x 3½in)

This card would work equally well for a birthday or even a retirement. Using the jelly letters allows you to create your own suitable text for the occasion.

To craft the card

Iron the adhesive on to the back of the stitching (see page 7). Cut out motif following the curves of the stitching and leaving a small amount of Aida showing all round (see page 7). Attach the design to the bottom of the card using mini glue dots. Use the jelly letters to spell out your chosen text, sticking them to the orange card. Trim the orange card around each word to give the effect of plant labels, then arrange above the motif and stick in place with glue dots.

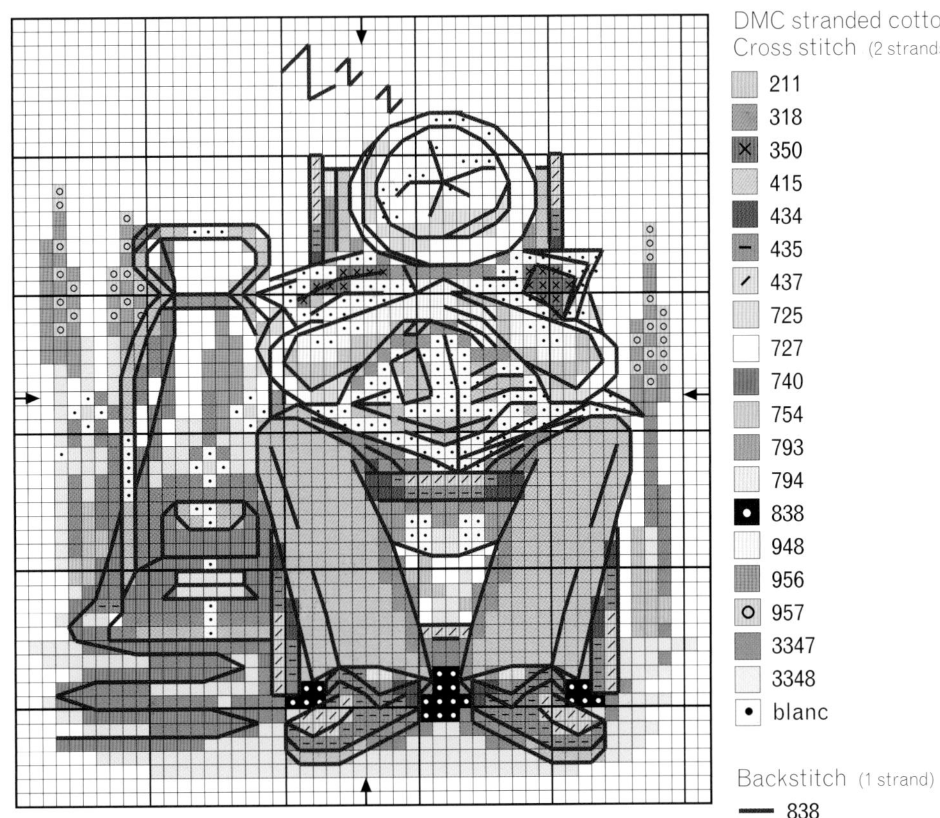

Star-Spangled Banner

You will need

28-count ice blue evenweave 13 x 15cm (5 x 6in)

DMC stranded cotton (floss) as listed in chart key

Double-fold card 105 x 150mm ($4\frac{1}{4}$ x 6in) in pearlescent silver

Iron-on adhesive

Piece of mulberry paper 10 x 12cm (4 x $4\frac{3}{4}$in) approx in navy blue

Six self-adhesive diamante stars 2mm ($\frac{1}{8}$in) and three diamante hearts 2mm ($\frac{1}{8}$in) – available in mixed pack

Three stick-on silver star sequins 1.25cm ($\frac{1}{2}$in)

Three red padded hearts 6mm ($\frac{1}{4}$in)

Small paintbrush

Mini glue dots

Stitch count 38h x 55w
Design size 6.9 x 10cm ($2\frac{3}{4}$ x 4in)

Note Remember to stitch over two threads of the evenweave fabric.

To craft the card

Iron the adhesive on to the back of the stitching (see page 7). Cut out leaving two or three threads of fabric all round. Use the paintbrush to damp the edges of the mulberry paper and tear the fibres away for a feathered effect. Use glue dots to attach the paper slightly to the left of the silver card. Stick the motif on top. Stick the three star sequins down the right side of the card, spacing evenly. Add a padded heart to the centre of each one using glue dots. Add the diamante hearts and stars to finish your card.

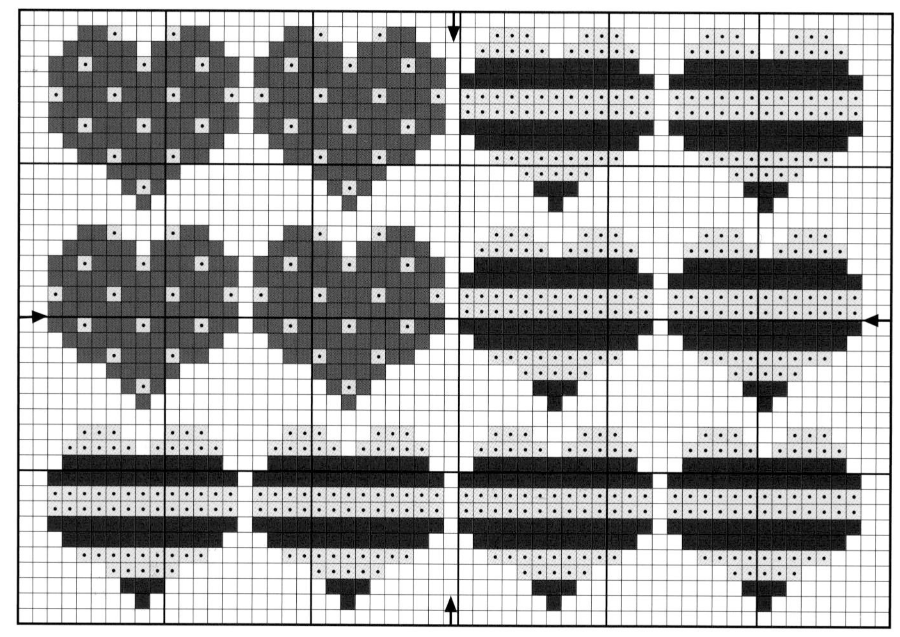

DMC stranded cotton
Cross stitch
(2 strands)

321
796
blanc

Hallowe'en Ghost

You will need

14-count white pearl-lustre Aida 13 x 15cm (5 x 6in)

DMC stranded cotton (floss) as listed in chart key

Single-fold card 105 x 150mm (4⅛ x 6in) in 'Vesuvius' glitter finish (see Suppliers)

Piece of card 10cm (4in) square in orange cord texture finish

Iron-on adhesive

Small moon-shaped punch (optional)

Small foam pads

Stitch count 46h x 36w
Design size 8.3 x 6.5cm (3¼ x 2½in)

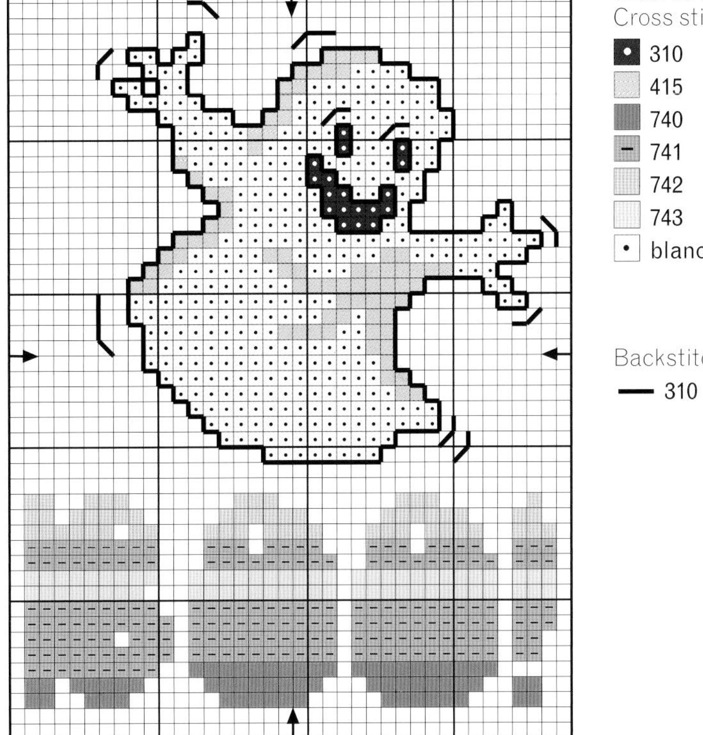

DMC stranded cotton
Cross stitch (2 strands)

- 310
- 415
- 740
- 741
- 742
- 743
- blanc

Backstitch (1 strand)

- 310

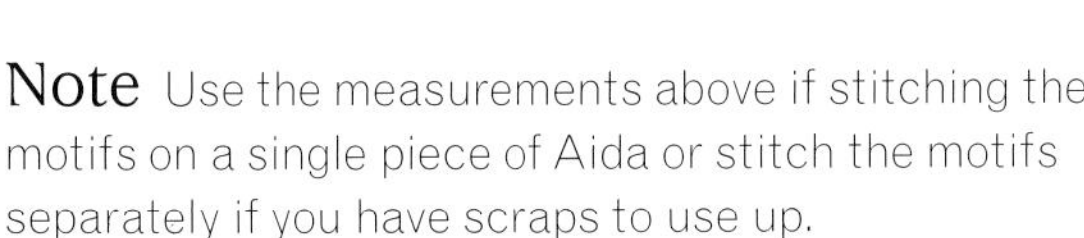

Note Use the measurements above if stitching the motifs on a single piece of Aida or stitch the motifs separately if you have scraps to use up.

To craft the card Iron the adhesive on to the back of the stitching (see page 7). Cut out the ghost and lettering following the design curves. Use a thin layer of clear glue to stick the ghost to the orange card. Allow to dry then cut around the motif, leaving a border of orange. Use small foam pads to stick the motif to the card, positioning it as shown (slightly scrape away the glitter where you are going to stick the motif). Attach the lettering with glue dots and punch out the moon embellishment and fix in place.

Hi Pumpkin!

I've enhanced the colours in this cute design by layering the motif on to fiery orange card. The purple glitter card makes a perfect backing, reflecting the design colours. Try stitching just the pumpkin and adding it to a small tag to make invitations for a Hallowe'en party.

Down the Chimney

You will need

14-count white Aida 13 x 20cm (5 x 8in)

DMC stranded cotton (floss) as listed in chart key

Double-fold card 100 x 210mm (4 x 8¼in) with triple apertures 45mm (1¾in) square in dark green linen effect

Self-adhesive ribbon 22cm (8¾in) long x 6mm (¼in) wide in red/green tartan

Two holly leaf sequins and berries or other embellishments

Double-sided tape and glue dots

Stitch count 84h x 24w
Design size 15.2 x 4.3cm (6 x 1¾in)

Note Use the measurements above if stitching on a single piece of Aida, or stitch the motifs separately if you have scraps to use up. If stitching on one piece leave about six squares of Aida between each motif (check measurement against your own card). The chart has blue dashed lines around each motif as a guide to positioning.

To craft the card Iron the adhesive on to the back of the stitching (see page 7). Mount into the aperture card as described on page 8. Stick the self-adhesive ribbon in place, as shown and finish by fixing the holly leaves and berries with glue dots.

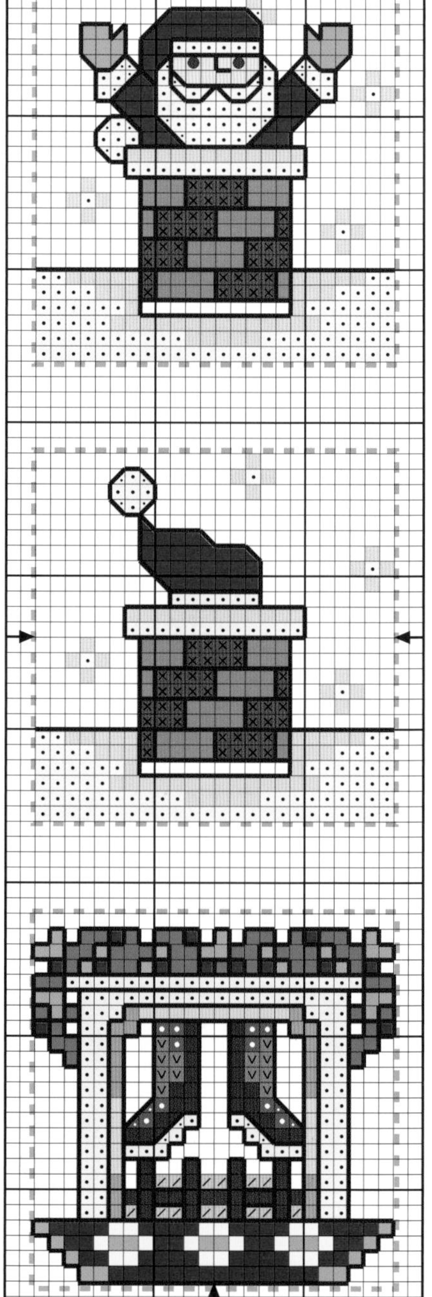

DMC stranded cotton
Cross stitch (2 strands)

- 340
- 341
- 349
- 434
- 435
- 699
- 702
- 727
- 742
- 754
- 838
- 920
- 922
- blanc

Backstitch (1 strand)
— 838

French knots (1 strand)
● 838

Indicates edges of motifs to aid placement in the aperture card. You could backstitch these lines in DMC 838

Present from Santa

I've given this quick-stitch card a special touch by adding a 'lid' and a red gingham ribbon trim, making it look like a gift box. On page 102 of More Card Ideas you'll find a selection of these motifs for speedy stitching. Make up a little stock of them in advance of the holiday so you always have something to hand to create last-minute cards.

Christmas Lights

You will need

14-count cream sparkle Aida with gold Lurex 13cm (5in) square

DMC stranded cotton (floss) as listed in chart key

Kreinik Blending Filament 091 pale yellow

Iron-on adhesive

Single-fold card 125mm (5in) square in bright red metallic

Piece of pearlescent card 8.5 x 9.5cm (3¼ x 3¾in) in pale gold

Self-adhesive ribbon 22cm (8¾in) long x 6mm (¼in) wide in red gingham

Four Christmas light embellishments (widely available, sometimes already on a string)

Gold metallic thread

Double-sided tape and mini glue dots

Stitch count 37h x 32w
Design size 6.7 x 5.8cm (2¾ x 2¼in)

To craft the card Iron the adhesive on to the back of the stitching (see page 7). Cut out the motif leaving about five squares of Aida all round. Cut two strips of gingham ribbon the same length as the Aida and stick on the fabric as shown. Repeat with two strips slightly larger than the Aida width. Fold surplus to the back. Use glue dots to stick the motif to the gold card and use double-sided tape to fix the whole thing on the card front. Thread a thin needle with about 40cm (16in) of gold thread. Leaving a small tail, pass the needle through the hole in one of the Christmas lights. Repeat to form a loop and pull tight, so the light is held securely. Repeat for the remaining lights leaving about 3cm (1¼in) of thread between each. Loop the gold thread around the fold of the card, pull tight so the lights hang at the front and secure by passing the needle through the hole in the first bulb, making a small knot. Trim thread ends neatly to finish.

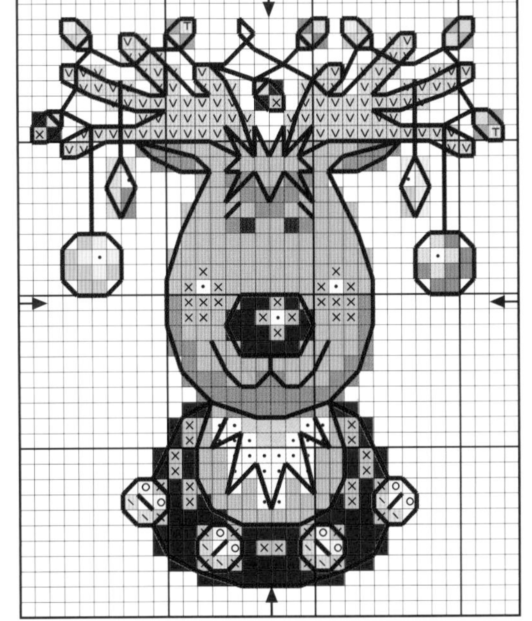

DMC stranded cotton
Cross stitch (2 strands)

- 209
- T 210
- 350
- × 352
- 415
- 436
- 437
- V 613
- 725
- 727
- 798
- 809
- 838
- 906
- 907
- • blanc

- ╲ 725 + Kreinik 091 (1 strand of each)
- O 727 + Kreinik 091 (1 strand of each)

Backstitch (1 strand)
— 838

Adorable Angel

You will need

- 14-count white Aida with pearl-lustre effect 13cm (5in) square
- DMC stranded cotton (floss) as listed in chart key
- Iron-on adhesive
- Rectangle of card 9 x 8cm (3½ x 3⅛in) in lilac
- Two pieces of spatter-foam mesh 10cm (4in) square in lilac
- Satin ribbon 18cm (7in) long x 6mm (¼in) wide in pale lilac polka dot
- Ready-made satin angel wings 3.5 x 10cm (1½ x 4in) in cream
- Needle and thread
- Double-sided tape and clear glue

Stitch count 33h x 35w
Design size 6 x 6.3cm (2⅜ x 2½in)

Stitch the angel in richer shades (charted page 101). Make your angel unique by adding beads and changing the fabric for her skirt. If you want to get the same billowing effect as the spatter-foam though you will need to use quite stiff fabric.

Note Use four strands of DMC 3341 to fill in the heart shapes on the cape using long stitch for a raised look. Work all areas of DMC 211 first, then work the long stitch. The hearts look equally pretty stitched in cross stitch or even beads.

To craft the card Iron the adhesive on to the back of the stitching (see page 7). Cut out the motif following the design shape. Remove the backing paper and cover the back with a thin layer of clear glue. To make the hanger, fold the ribbon in half and stick the ends into the glue. Press the angel down on to the piece of card so the ribbon hangs free. When dry, trim excess card. To make the skirt, trim the lower edges of the spatter-foam mesh in a curve. Place the pieces together and starting 6mm (¼in) from the top edge run a gathering stitch through them. Gather until the mesh measures about 2.5cm (1in), secure with a few stitches and push the gathers into a bell shape. Stick the skirt to the back of the angel using double-sided tape (at a slight angle to give a billowing effect). Attach her wings to finish.

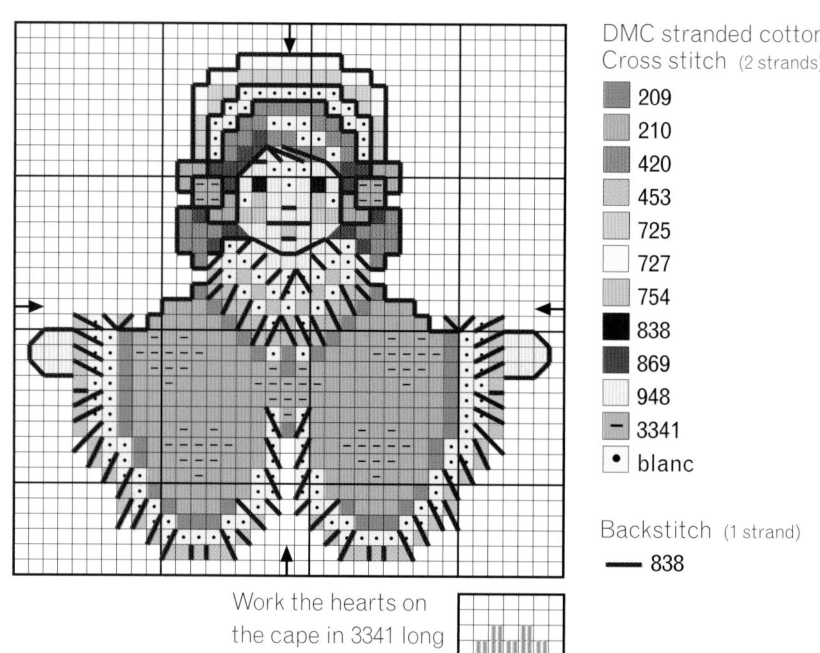

Work the hearts on the cape in 3341 long stitches if you prefer

Three Wise Men

You will need

28-count antique cream evenweave 15cm (6in) square

DMC stranded cotton (floss) as listed in chart key

Single-fold card 148mm (5¾in) square in cobalt blue

Iron-on adhesive

Mini glue dots

Peel-off filigree star (from pack) 3.5cm (1¼in) in gold

Stitch count 56h x 54w
Design size 10 x 9.8cm (4 x 3¾in)

Note Remember to stitch over two threads of the evenweave fabric.

To craft the card

Iron the adhesive on to the back of the stitching (see page 7). Cut out following the curves of the design leaving about 6mm (¼in) of evenweave all round. Use mini glue dots to stick the motif slightly to the left side of the card and about 1.25cm (½in) from the lower edge. Stick on the filigree star at top right.

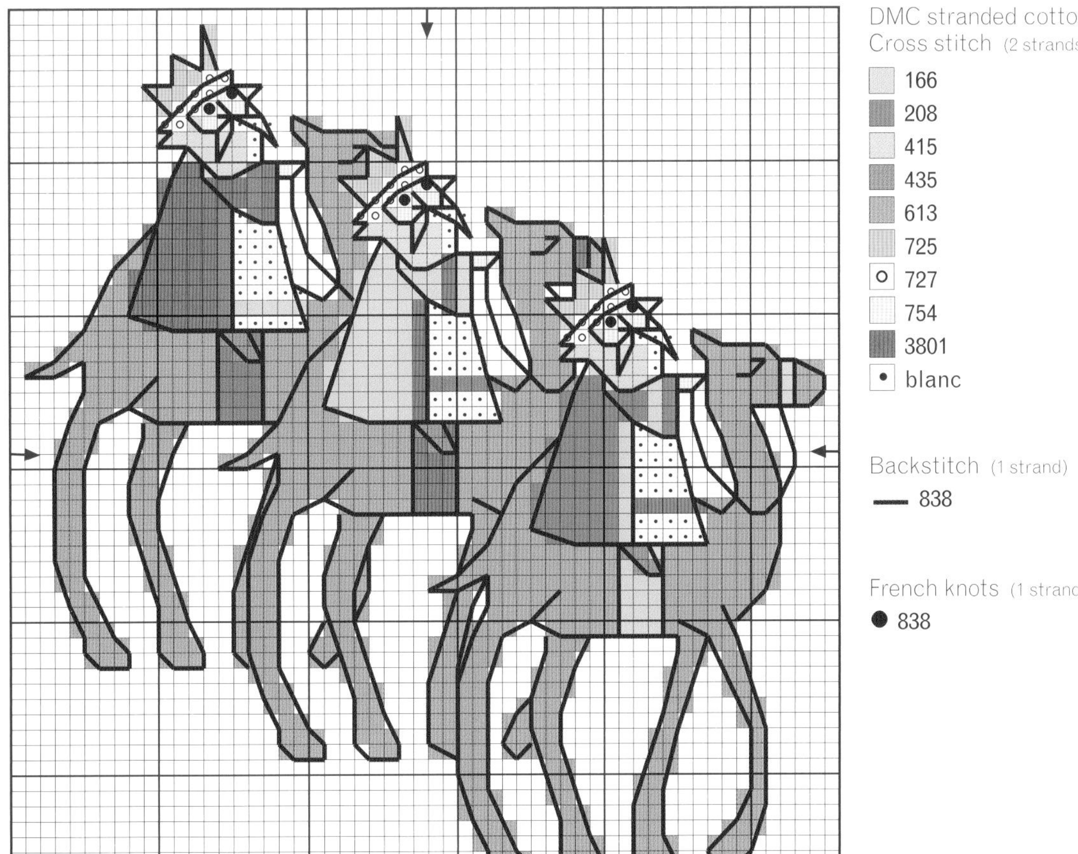

DMC stranded cotton
Cross stitch (2 strands)

- 166
- 208
- 415
- 435
- 613
- 725
- 727
- 754
- 3801
- blanc

Backstitch (1 strand)

- 838

French knots (1 strand)

- 838

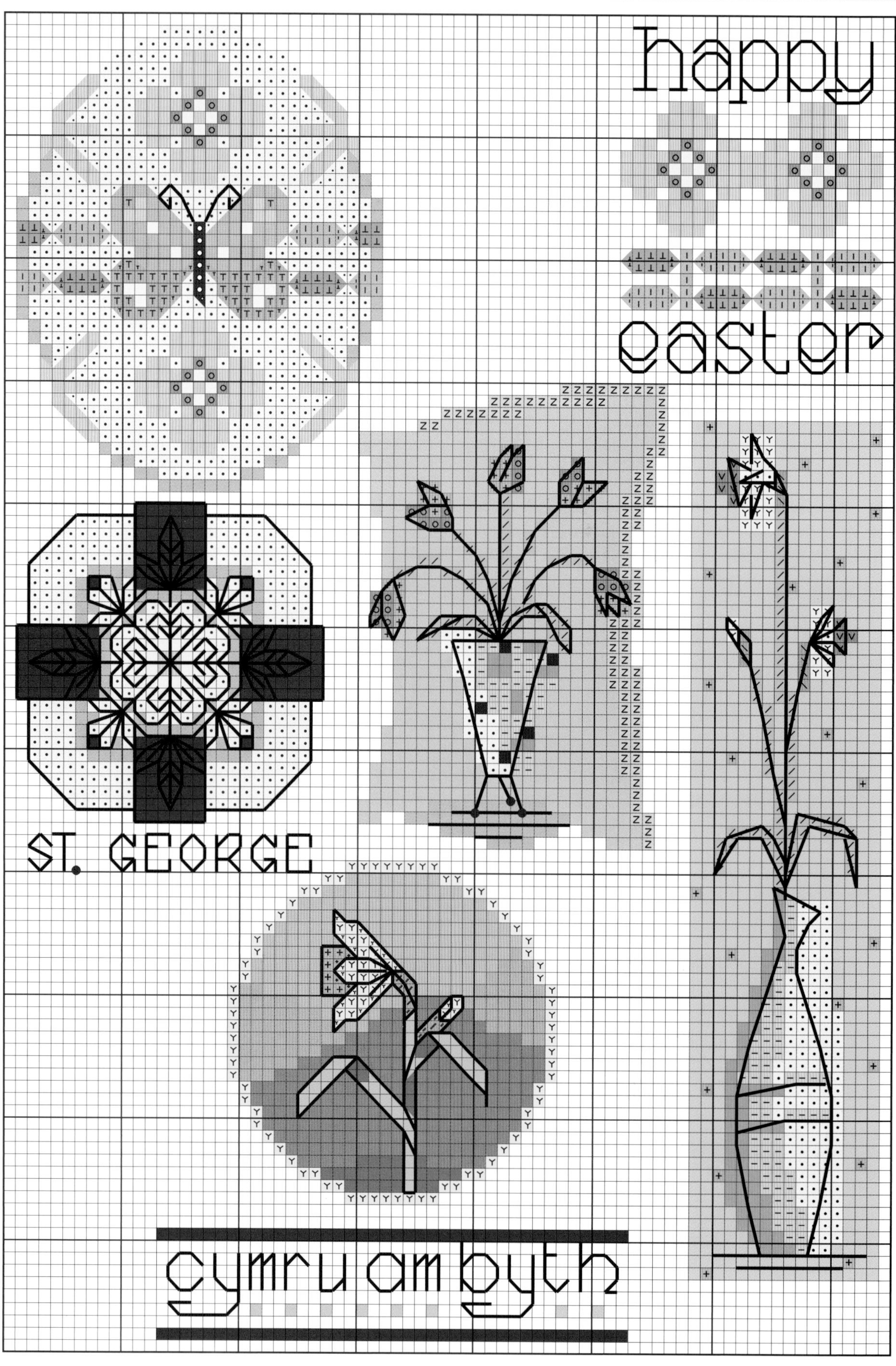
happy
easter
ST. GEORGE
cymru am byth

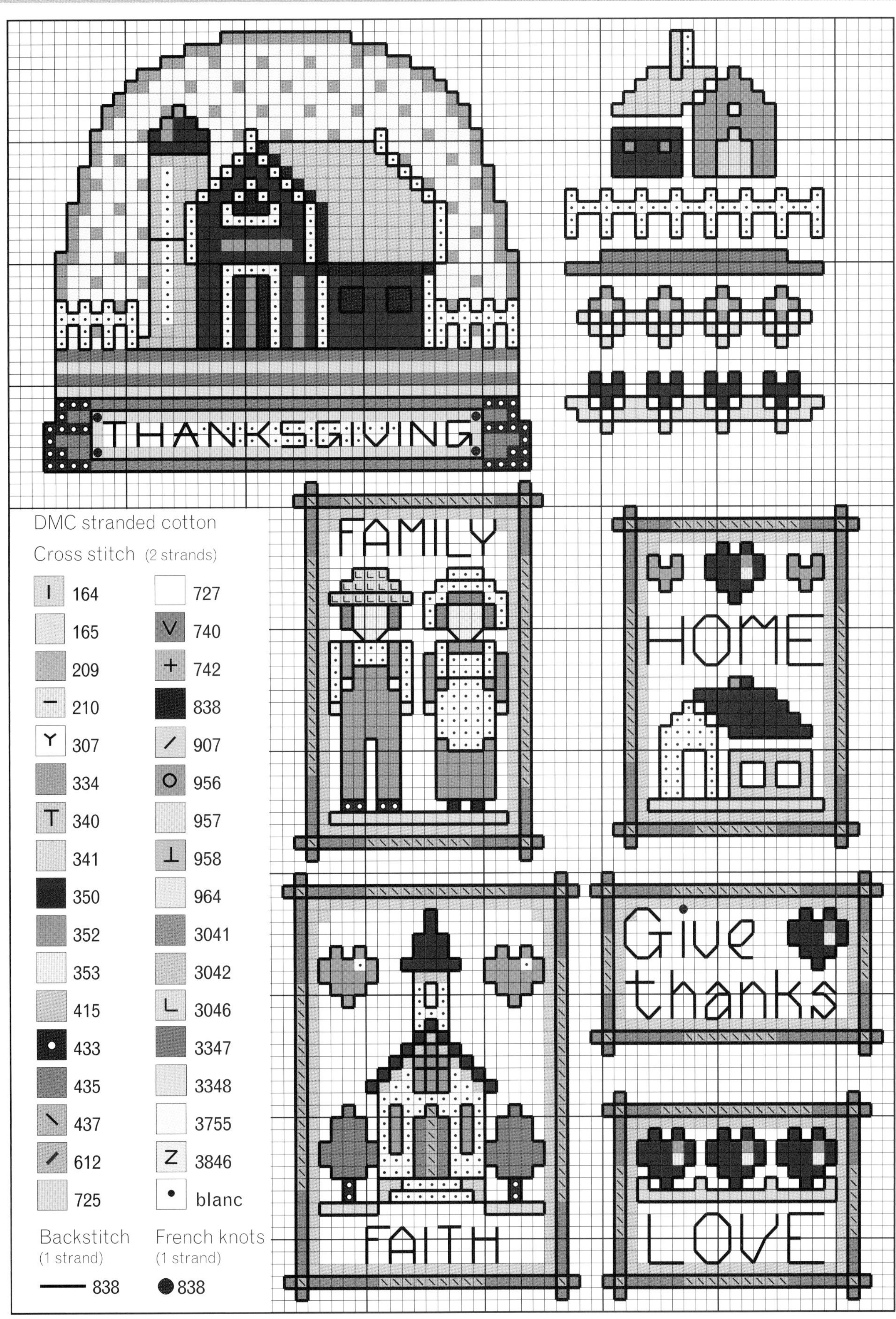
THANKSGIVING
FAMILY
HOME
Give thanks
FAITH
LOVE
DMC stranded cotton
Cross stitch (2 strands)
164
165
209
210
307
334
340
341
350
352
353
415
433
435
437
612
725
727
740
742
838
907
956
957
958
964
3041
3042
3046
3347
3348
3755
3846
blanc
Backstitch (1 strand)
838
French knots (1 strand)
838

HI PUMPKIN!
Come to a Wizard Party!
HUBBLE
BUBBLE
Scary or What?

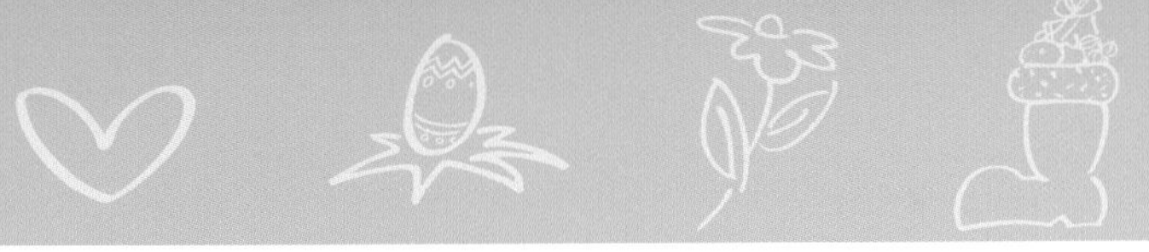

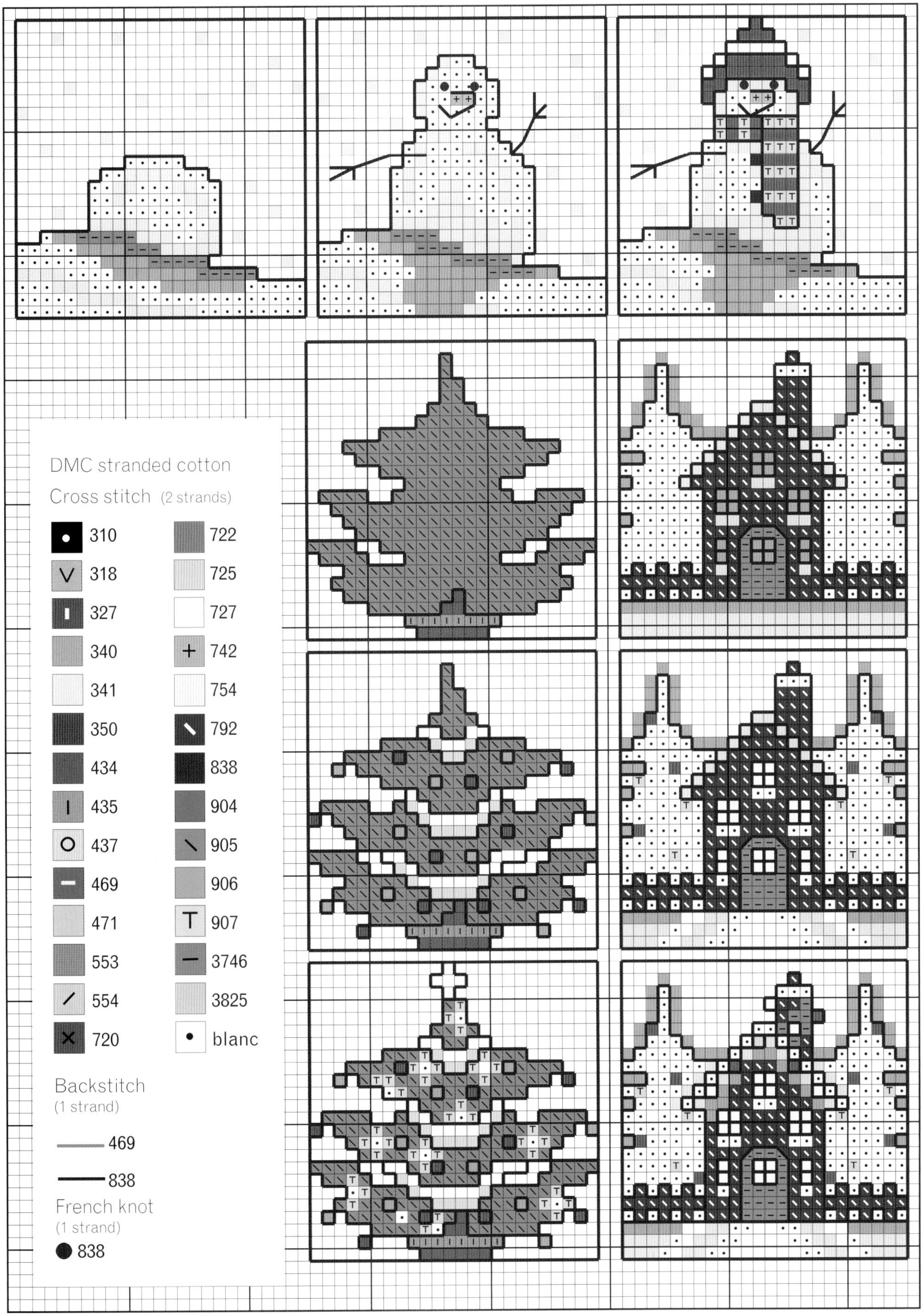

DMC stranded cotton

Cross stitch (2 strands)

•	310		722
V	318		725
I	327		727
	340	+	742
	341		754
	350	\	792
	434		838
I	435		904
O	437	\	905
–	469		906
	471	T	907
	553	–	3746
/	554		3825
X	720	•	blanc

Backstitch (1 strand)

469

838

French knot (1 strand)

● 838

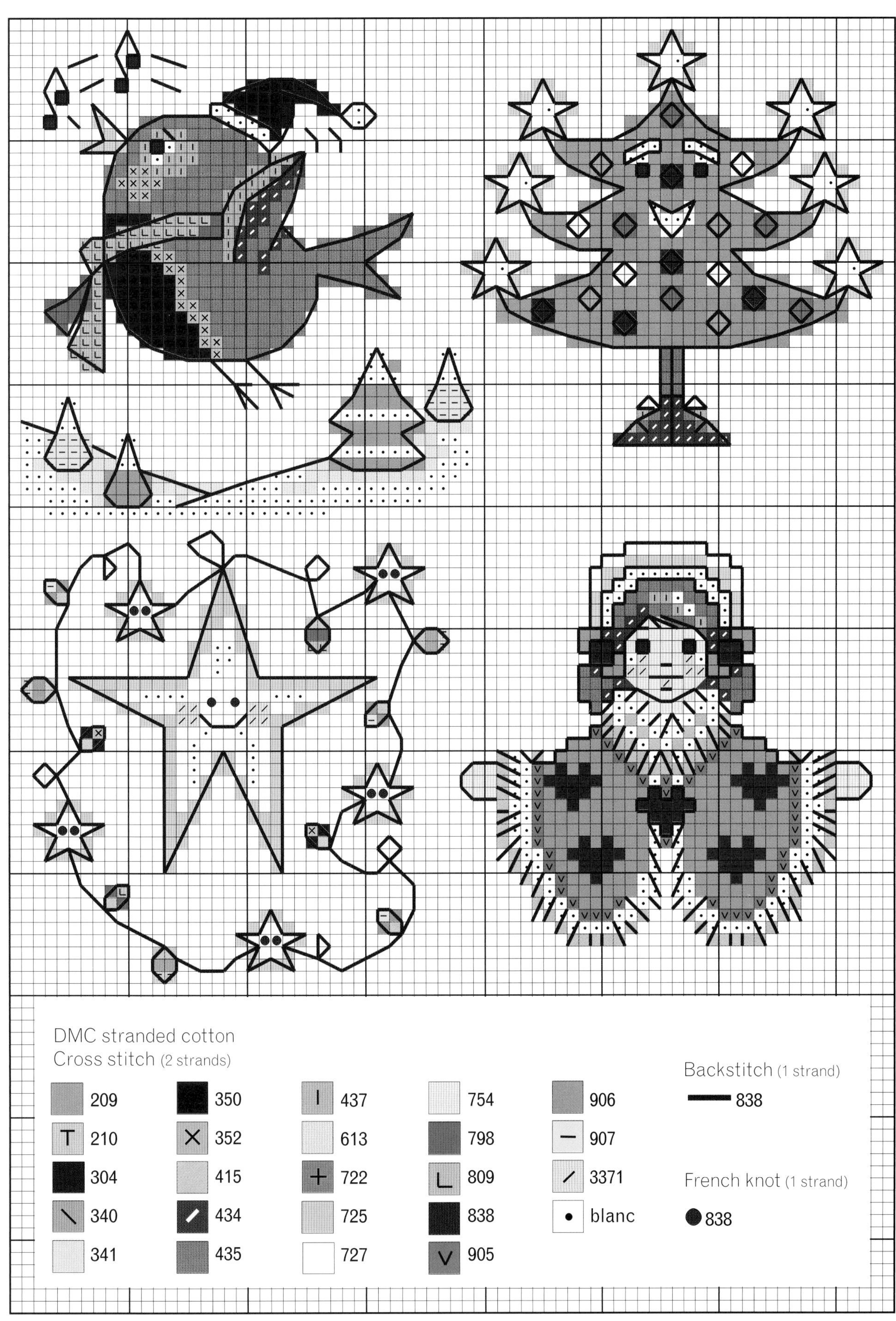
DMC stranded cotton
Cross stitch (2 strands)
209
T 210
304
340
341
350
352
415
434
435
437
613
722
725
727
754
798
809
838
905
906
907
3371
blanc
Backstitch (1 strand)
838
French knot (1 strand)
838

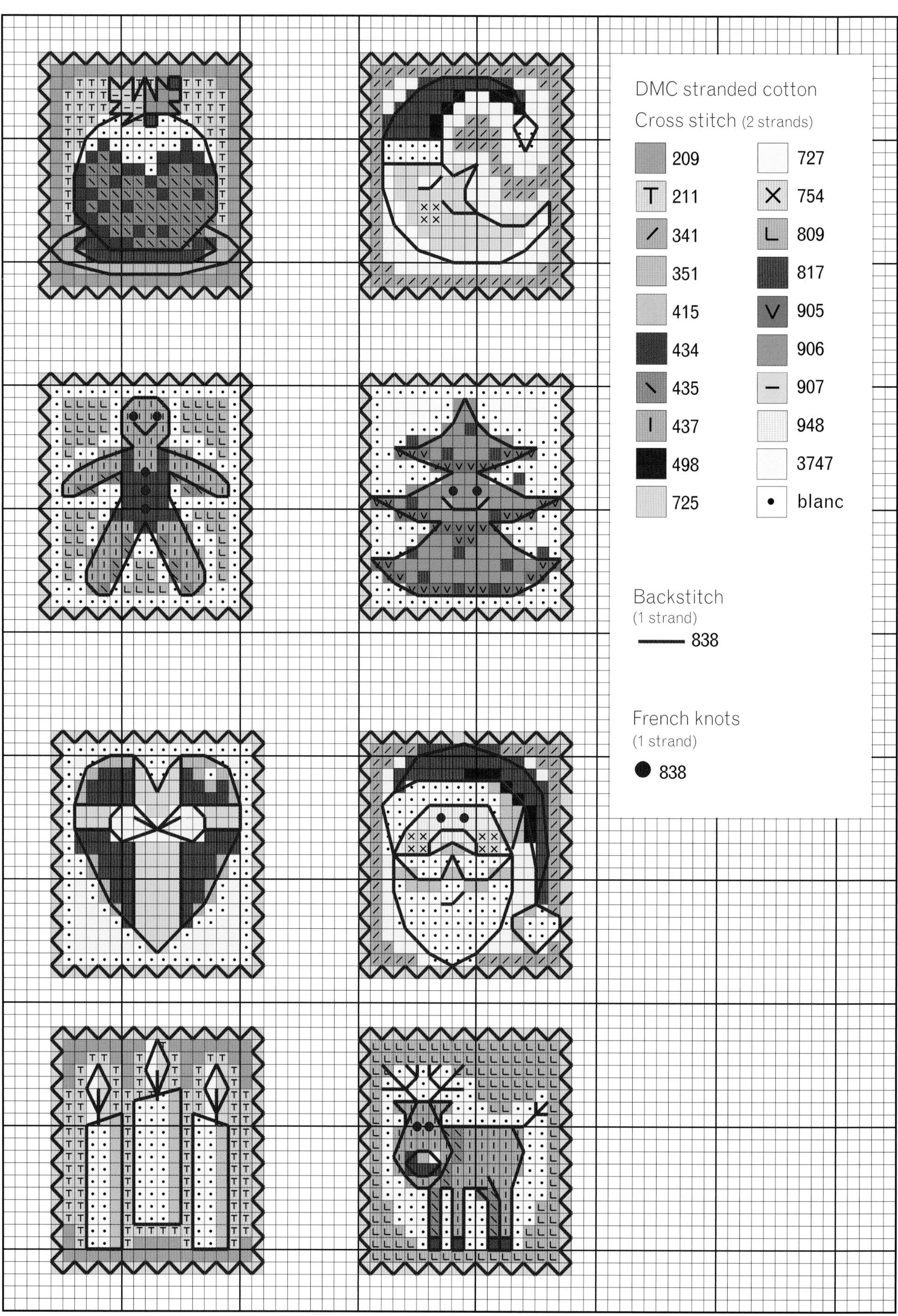
DMC stranded cotton
Cross stitch (2 strands)
209
T 211
/ 341
351
415
434
\ 435
I 437
498
725
727
× 754
L 809
817
V 905
906
– 907
948
3747
• blanc
Backstitch
(1 strand)
838
French knots
(1 strand)
838

DMC stranded cotton
Cross stitch (2 strands)
817
Backstitch
(1 strand)
498
838
French knots
(1 strand)
838

Suppliers

UK

Artymiss
51 Huggetts Lane, Eastbourne, East Sussex
BN22 0LT, UK
tel: 020 7193 7293; fax: 0870 235 1790
www.artymiss.co.uk
For card and paper craft supplies

Monika Carrie Design
West Haybogs, Tough/Alford, Aberdeenshire
AB33 8DU, UK
www.quilting-and-stitching.co.uk
For felt

Coats Crafts
PO Box 22, Lingfield House, McMullen Road,
Darlington, Co. Durham DL1 1YQ, UK
tel: 01325 394237; fax: 01325 394200
www.coatscrafts.co.uk
For cross stitch supplies and Anchor threads

Craft Creations
Ingersoll House, Delamere Road, Cheshunt,
Herts EN8 9HD, UK
tel: 01992 781900; fax: 01992 634339
www.craftcreations.co.uk
For card and paper craft supplies

Craftee
98 Brookfield Walk, Clevedon, Somerset
BS21 9YJ, UK
tel: 0709 201 2386
www.craftee.co.uk
For card and paper craft supplies

Craftwork Cards Limited
Unit 2, The Moorings, Waterside Road,
Stourton, Leeds LS10 1RW, UK
tel: 0113 2765713 / 2705986
www.craftworkcards.co.uk
For card and paper supplies including 'apple fizz' and 'Vesuvius' glitter cards, and 'vino', 'elf' and 'fairy' cord texture cards

DMC (UK)
DMC Creative World, Pullman Road, Wigston,
Leicester LE18 2DY, UK
tel: 01162 811040 www.dmc.com
For cross stitch supplies

Get Crafty
7 Ordnance Road, Southampton, Hants
SO15 2AZ, UK
tel: 023 8023 3074; fax: 08700 524220
www.getcrafty.co.uk
For card and paper craft supplies and keepsake albums

HobbyCraft (stores across UK)
tel: 01452 424999
www.hobbycraft.co.uk
For general craft supplies

Impress Cards
Slough Farm, Westhall, Halesworth, Suffolk
IP19 8RN, UK
tel: 01986 781422; fax: 01986 781677
www.impress-cards.co.uk
For card and paper craft supplies

Memory Keepsakes
Shakeford Mill, Hinstock, Market Drayton,
Shropshire, TF9 2SP, UK
tel: 01630 638342; Fax: 01630 639867
www.memorykeepsakes.co.uk
For card and paper craft supplies and albums

Panduro Hobby (mail order)
Westway House, Transport Avenue,
Brentford, Middlesex TW8 9HF, UK
tel: 08702 422 878 (orders)
www.panduro.co.uk
For general craft supplies, including cardboard and plastic hearts, acrylic boxes, wooden trinket boxes and brooch backs

Paperarts
Toadsmoor Road, Brimscombe, Stroud,
Gloucestershire GL5 2TB, UK
tel: 01453 886038
www.paperarts.co.uk
For card and paper craft supplies

Scrapbooks by J
53 Henthorn Road, Clitheroe, Lancashire
BB7 2LD, UK
www.scrapbookingcastle.co.uk
For the circular mini book

Scrapbook Mad
PO Box 10731, Birmingham, B27 6YB, UK
www.scrapbookmad.co.uk
For card and paper craft supplies, mulberry paper, mini albums, including K & Co mini book (code SKUKC535527)

A Treasured Memory
Boscombe Enterprise Centre, Unit 1,
Station Approach, Ashley Road,
Boscombe BH1 4NB, UK
www.atreasuredmemory.co.uk
For card and paper craft supplies

USA

Joann Stores, Inc (stores across USA)
5555 Darrow Road, Hudson Ohio, USA
tel: 1 888 739 4120
email: guest service@jo-annstores.com
www.joann.com
For general needlework and craft supplies

Kreinik Manufacturing Company, Inc
3106 Timanus Lane, Suite 101, Baltimore,
MD 21244, USA
tel: 1800 537 2166 www.kreinik.com
For metallic threads and blending filaments

MCG Textiles
13845 Magnolia Avenue, Chino,
CA 91710, USA
tel: 909 591-6351 www.mcgtextiles.com
For cross stitch supplies

M & J Buttons
1000 Sixth Avenue, New York, NY 10018, USA
tel: 212 391 6200 www.mjtrim.com
For beads, buttons, ribbons and trimmings

Mill Hill, a division of Wichelt Imports Inc
N162 Hwy 35, Stoddard WI 54658, USA
tel: 608 788 4600; fax: 608 788 6040
www. millhill.com
For beads, charms and buttons

Yarn Tree Designs
PO Box 724, Ames, Iowa 500100724, USA
tel: 1 800 247 3952 www.yarntree.com
For cross stitch supplies and card mounts

About the Author

Sue Cook has been a freelance designer since 1992 and has worked for many of the major UK stitching magazines, creating hundreds of designs. This is Sue's fifth book, having previously written *Cross Stitch Inspirations*, *Sue Cook's Wonderful Cross Stitch Collection*, *Sue Cook's Bumper Cross Stitch Collection* and *Sue Cook's Christmas Cross Stitch Collection*. Sue lives in Newport, South Wales.

Acknowledgments

My love and thanks go, as always, to my wonderful and ever-supportive family, especially my very own grumpy but lovable old man, Ade, who was there on the days when I felt my heart was breaking. To my friend and commissioning editor Cheryl Brown at David & Charles, for allowing me a few 'elasticated' deadlines to get the job done! I'm also indebted to everyone else who has played a part in the production of this book, in particular Lin Clements who cheerfully edits my charts and text with such skill and care. Thanks to Daphne White for stitching most of the projects in Memorable Days and Jennifer Williams who during difficult days for her family still found time and energy to stitch for me. A book like this would be impossible without their loyal help.

As always I'd like to thank Cara Ackerman and everyone at DMC for their continued support and for supplying beautiful fabrics and threads to me. Thanks to Sue and her staff at Craftworks Cards in Leeds, who provided inspiration with their gorgeous range of cards and other goodies. The generosity of these suppliers is much appreciated.

Finally, I'd like to thank the editors of several stitching magazines who have put up with me turning down most of their commissions for the past year because of this book! They have been the bedrock of my career as a professional designer and I value their continuing support and friendship.

Index